CHOPSTICKS RECIPES

INTRODUCTION

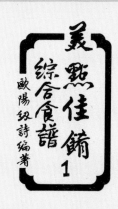

美點佳餚
綜合食譜 1
歐陽玆詩編著

Published and Distributed by
Chopsticks Publications Ltd.
P.O. Box 73515, Kowloon Central Post Office, Kowloon, Hong Kong.
108 Boundary St., G/F, Kowloon, Hong Kong.
Tel.: 336 8433   339 0454
Fax: (852) 336 8287

ISBN 962 7018 61 9
Photography by Au-yeung Chiu Mei
Edited by Caroline Au-yeung

UK Sole Distributor:
Gazelle Book Services Ltd
Falcon House Queen Square
Lancaster LA1 1RN
England

出版者及總批發
嘉饌出版有限公司

香港　九龍中央郵箱73515號
香港　九龍界限街108號地下
電話：336 8433、339 0454
傳眞：（852）336 8287
本書版權所有不得翻印或轉載

FOREWORD

When my recipes first appeared in local periodicals and magazines, many readers wrote to me saying that it was quite inconvenient for them to collect my recipes one by one. They suggested that I should publish a book. The same requisition was made by my students. The idea was more than appealing. Therefore, I decided to publish a series of cookbooks, instead of just one, under my personal supervision. I have done my best to present them in an understandable, easy-to-follow pattern.

All my recipes were tested and re-tested by myself, my assistants and my students in our fully-equipped kitchen. They are workable recipes illustrated with tempting, colourful pictures taken by our professional photographer, as it is my firm belief that seeing is better than reading.

Most people are afraid to attempt Chinese cookery because of the elaborate preparation, materials and utensils that are required. If you try these recipes, you will find that they are easy-to-follow and can be done in any ordinary western kitchen. So, why not make these mouth-watering dishes yourself to be served steaming hot from your own kitchen and be a money-saver at the same time?

All our staff at the Chopsticks Cooking Centre will gladly answer your cooking queries if you phone or write to us.

This book, as well as the subsequent books under the 'Chopsticks Recipes' title are offered to those who like Chinese cookery. We hope that you will enjoy the cooking as much as the dishes themselves.

Cecilia J. Au-yang

3

CONTENTS

目 錄

7

好 市 發 財

Braised Dried Oysters with Black Moss

材料：

蠔豉5安（140克）
髮菜½安（14克）
紅蘿蔔數片
油2湯匙
羌2片
葱頭2粒

醃料—糖½茶匙　　調味—上湯2杯
　　　胡椒粉少許　　　　酒1茶匙
　　　水1湯匙　　　　　蠔油2茶匙
　　　　　　　　　　　　糖1茶匙
　　　　　　　　　　　　生粉水1湯匙
　　　　　　　　　　　　老抽數滴

製法：

* 蠔豉洗淨浸30分鐘後隔去水份，排放在深碟內，加入醃料拌勻醃20分鐘。置蒸籠內以中火蒸30分鐘至軟，取出隔乾水份。
* 髮菜洗淨浸透與紅蘿蔔片一同放入沸水中飛水，撈起過冷河隔去水份。髮菜再用上湯1杯煮1分鐘。取出揸乾水份。上湯棄去。將髮菜放在蠔豉上。
* 燒紅鑊加油1湯匙，爆香一半羌片及葱頭後棄去。讚酒½茶匙倒下上湯½杯及一半調味料煮沸。隨即倒在髮菜及蠔豉上，置蒸籠內蒸5分鐘。倒出蠔豉汁留用。將髮菜蠔豉反倒在平碟上。以紅蘿蔔片點綴。
* 鑊再燒熱加入另1湯匙油煮沸，爆香其餘羌片及葱頭後棄去。讚下餘酒、上湯、蠔豉汁及調味料煮沸，以生粉水埋饙饛淋在蠔豉面即可上桌。

Ingredients:

5 oz (140 g) dried oysters
1/2 oz (14 g) black moss
2 cups boiling water
4 slices carrot
2 tbsp oil
2 slices ginger
2 shallots

Oyster Marinade-
1/2 tsp sugar
1/8 tsp pepper
1 tbsp water

Seasoning-
2 cups stock
1 tsp wine
2 tsp oyster sauce
1 tsp sugar

Gravy Mix-
1 tsp cornflour
1 tbsp water
1/4 tsp dark soy

Method:

* Wash and soak the dried oyster for 30 minutes. Discard the water and arrange the oysters in a deep saucer. Mix the marinade then pour over the oysters and leave to stand for 20 minutes. Steam over moderate heat for 30 minutes or until soft. Drain and leave aside for later use.
* Wash and soak the black moss. Blanch in the boiling water with the carrot, refresh and drain.

Pour in 1 cup of the stock and simmer for 1 minute. Remove and squeeze to dry. Discard the stock then arrange the black moss over the oysters.

* Heat the wok with 1 tbsp of the oil to sauté half of the ginger and shallots then discard. Sizzle half of the wine and pour in 1/2 cup stock and seasoning to bring to boil. Pour over the black moss and oysters. Steam again for 5 minutes. Remove and drain out the juice for later use. Invert the saucer to pour the oysters and black moss on a platter. Garnish with the carrot.

* Reheat the wok with the other tbsp of oil to sauté the remaining ginger and shallot then discard. Add the rest of the wine, stock, juice and the seasoning to bring to the boil. Thicken the sauce with the gravy mix then pour over the dish and serve hot.

恭　喜　發　財

Braised Mushrooms
with Black Moss

材料：

花菇2安（56克） 調味─上湯1½杯
髮菜½安（14克） 酒½茶匙
紅蘿蔔數片 蠔油2茶匙
白菜6安（168克） 糖1茶匙
油3湯匙 胡椒粉少許
鹽1湯匙 生粉水1湯匙
羌1片 老抽數滴
葱頭2粒

醃料─鹽¼茶匙
　　　糖½茶匙
　　　油1茶匙

製法：

* 冬菇洗淨以清水浸軟，剪去菇蒂，
  揸乾水份。加入醃料中醃10分鐘。
  雞膏舖上置籠內蒸15分鐘，取出棄
  去雞膏。
* 髮菜預先浸1小時發透洗淨，與紅
  蘿蔔片一同置沸水中飛水，隔乾水
  份。沸水留用。
* 上湯一杯煮沸，放下髮菜煨3分鐘
  ，隔去水份。
* 白菜洗淨置上述沸水中加油1湯匙
  及鹽略拖，揸乾水份圍放碟旁。
* 髮菜放入油鑊中加油1湯匙一翻，
  隨即盛起排在碟中央。
* 再燒紅鑊加餘油爆香羌、葱頭後棄
  去。倒入冬菇兜炒20秒鐘，讚酒加
  其餘上湯及調味料，蓋上鑊蓋煮30
  秒鐘。以生粉水埋饙和勻盛在碟中
  ，加紅蘿蔔片點綴。

1 slice ginger
2 shallots

Marinade-	Seasoning-
1/4 tsp salt	1 1/2 cups stock
1/2 tsp sugar	1/2 tsp wine
1 tsp oil	2 tsp oyster sauce
	1 tsp sugar
	1/8 tsp pepper
	1 tbsp cornflour mix
	1/4 tsp dark soy

Ingredients:

2 oz (56 g) Chinese mushrooms
1 piece chicken fat
1/2 oz (14 g) black moss
2 cups boiling water
10 pieces carrot
6 oz (168 g) Chinese cabbages
3 tbsp oil
1 tbsp salt

Method:

* Wash and soak the mushrooms till soft. Remove the stalks and squeeze to dry. Immerse in the marinade for 10 minutes. Cover with the chicken fat and steam for 15 minutes. Remove and discard the fat.
* Soak the black moss for an hour. Wash and blanch in the boiling water with the carrot then drain. Keep the boiling water.
* Bring 1 cup of the stock to boil. Add the black moss to simmer for 3 minutes. Drain.
* Wash and blanch the cabbages in the above boiling water with 1 tbsp of the oil and the salt. Drain and arrange round the edge of the platter.
* Reheat the black moss in the wok with 1 tbsp of the oil then arrange in the centre of the platter.
* Heat the wok with the remaining oil. Saute the ginger and shallots till fragrant and discard. Pour in the mushrooms to stir fry for 20 seconds. Sizzle the wine and add the remaining stock and the seasoning. Cover and simmer for 30 seconds. Thicken the stock with the gravy mix. Dish and garnish with the carrot.

白 津 茸 腿

Celery Cabbage in Ham Sauce

材料：

黃芽白1½磅（¾公斤）
火腿2安（56克）
水4杯
油4湯匙
鹽2湯匙
雞粉1茶匙

調味—酒1茶匙
　　　上湯½杯
　　　蠔油1湯匙
　　　糖1茶匙
　　　胡椒粉少許
饡料—生粉1茶匙
　　　水1湯匙
　　　老抽¼茶匙
　　　蔴油1茶匙

製法：

* 將黃芽白洗淨，撕去硬脈，用剪刀修好。
* 火腿剁成茸候用。
* 鑊內放水煮沸後，加入油2湯匙、鹽、雞粉及黃芽白煨2分鐘至軟。
* 用罩籬把菜撈起隔去水份，排在長碟上。
* 燒紅鑊加入餘油，潷酒倒入上湯及調味料煮沸。生粉與水及老抽和勻流入打饡，淋在黃芽白上，火腿茸洒在上面即可。

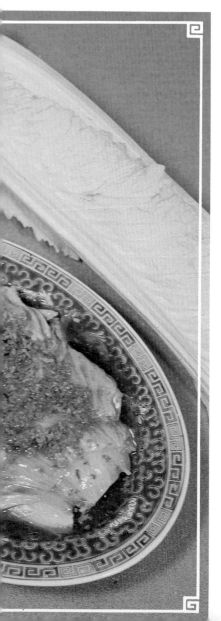

Ingredients:

1½ lb (¾ kg) celery cabbage
2 oz (56 g) Virginia ham
4 cups water
4 tbsp oil
2 tbsp salt
1 tsp chicken powder

Seasoning-
1 tsp sherry
½ cup stock
1 tbsp oyster sauce
1 tsp sugar
⅛ tsp pepper

Gravy Mix-
1 tsp cornflour
1 tbsp water
¼ tsp dark soy
1 tsp sesame oil

Method:

* Wash and trim the cabbage.
* Finely chop the ham.
* Bring the water to boil in the wok. Add 2 tbsp of the oil, the salt and the chicken powder to cook the cabbage for 2 minutes or until tender.
* Drain the cabbage well. Squeeze out the excess water then arrange on an oval platter.
* Bring the remaining oil to boil in a heated wok. Sizzle the sherry, add the stock and seasoning to bring to the boil again. Thicken the sauce with the gravy mix; pour over the cabbage and garnish with the minced ham.

13

蒜子柱甫

Dried Scallops with Garlic

材料：

瑤柱8安（224克）
水1杯
蒜頭6安（168克）
沸油3杯
雞膏1塊
菜薳8安（224克）
沸水2杯
油3湯匙
鹽1湯匙

調味—糖½茶匙　餡料—生粉1茶匙
　　　紹酒1茶匙　　　水1湯匙
　　　瑤柱水½杯　　　蠔油1茶匙
　　　胡椒粉少許

製法：

* 瑤柱洗淨放碟上，將水注入約¼吋（0.5公分）高浸1小時，反轉再浸1小時。
* 蒜頭去衣後放入猛油鑊中炸至金黃色候用。
* 將瑤柱排在淺碗中，加入餘水，置蒸籠內蒸30分鐘倒起瑤柱水留用。
* 將一半糖、蒜頭、雞膏放在瑤柱上再蒸30分鐘，雞膏棄去。
* 菜薳洗淨後放在沸水中加油1湯匙及鹽煨片刻。隔去水份，排在碟中。瑤柱水隔乾反轉倒在時菜上。
* 餘油放在熱鑊中，潷酒加瑤柱上湯煮滾，試妥味以生粉水及蠔油埋餡，淋在瑤柱上即成。

Ingredients:

8 oz (224 g) dried scallops
1 cup water
6 oz (168 g) garlic
3 cups hot oil
1 piece chicken fat
8 oz (224 g) green vegetables
2 cups boiling water
3 tbsp oil
1 tbsp salt

Seasoning-
1/2 tsp sugar
1 tsp wine
1/2 cup scallop water
1/8 tsp pepper

Gravy Mix-
1 tsp cornflour
1 tbsp water
1 tsp oyster sauce

Method:

* Wash and soak the scallops in 1/4" (0.5 cm) of the water for an hour. Turn and soak the other side for another hour.
* Peel and deep fry the garlic in the hot oil until golden brown. Leave aside for later use.
* Arrange the scallops in a shallow bowl. Add the remaining water to steam for 30 minutes then drain the water and keep as stock.
* Sprinkle half of the sugar and put the garlic and chicken fat on top of the scallops to steam for another 30 minutes. Discard the chicken fat.

* Wash and blanch the green vegetables in the boiling water with 1 tbsp of the oil and salt. Squeeze out the excess water and arrange on a platter. Drain the liquid in the bowl and turn it upside down on top of the vegetables.

* Heat the wok with the remaining oil. Sizzle the wine and bring the scallop stock to boil. Season to taste. Thicken the juice with the gravy mix. Pour over the scallops and serve hot.

京 都 排 骨
Pork Chops in Sweet and Sour Sauce

材料：

排骨10安（280克）
熱油3杯
番茄1只
番茜2棵
酒1茶匙

醃料—生抽1茶匙	饋料—茄汁1湯匙
生粉1茶匙	喼汁1茶匙
五香粉1茶匙	浙醋2茶匙
南乳1茶匙	生抽1茶匙
糖1茶匙	糖1茶匙
酒1茶匙	生粉1茶匙
水3湯匙	上湯½杯
	紅粉少許

製法：

* 排骨洗淨浸在已和勻之醃料中醃1小時。
* 燒紅鑊加油慢火煮沸，將排骨放入以大火炸至金黃色。取出隔去餘油斬件，鑊中留下2湯匙油候用。
* 番茄切片，番茜洗淨摘妥。
* 饋料全部和勻，燒紅鑊加油1½湯匙。讚酒倒下饋料煮沸，將排骨放入鑊中兜勻。加入尾油½湯匙拌勻上碟，以番茄片及番茜點綴。

Ingredients:

10 oz (280 g) pork chops
3 cups hot oil
1 tomato
2 parsley sprigs
1 tsp sherry

Marinade-
1 tsp light soy
1 tsp cornflour
1 tsp five spice powder
1 tsp preserved red bean curd
1 tsp sugar
1 tsp wine
3 tbsp water

Gravy Mix-
1 tbsp tomato ketchup
1 tsp OK sauce
2 tsp red vinegar
1 tsp light soy
1 tsp sugar
1 tsp cornflour
¹/₂ cup stock
¹/₄ tsp red food colouring

Method:

* *Clean and immerse the pork chops in the marinade for 1 hour.*
* *Slowly bring the oil to the boil in a heated wok. Deep fry the pork chops over high heat till golden brown. Remove, drain and chop into bite-sized pieces. Keep 2 tbsp oil for later use.*
* *Slice the tomato. Wash and trim the parsley.*
* *Mix all the gravy ingredients together then heat a wok with 1¹/₂ tbsp of the oil. Sizzle the sherry, add the gravy and bring to boil. Return the pork chops into the wok to coat each piece evenly with the sauce. Add the last ¹/₂ tbsp of oil to mix well. Dish and garnish with the tomato slices and parsley.*

仙 掌 魚 唇

Stewed Duck's Webs
with Fish Maw

材料：

雪藏魚唇½磅（224克）
羌3片
酒1湯匙
鴨腳16隻　　　　調味—鹽½茶匙
老抽2湯匙　　　　　　酒1湯匙
沸油4杯　　　　　　　生抽1茶匙
八角3粒　　　　　　　蠔油1茶匙
花椒½茶匙　　　　　　糖½茶匙
陳皮1方吋　　　　　　胡椒粉少許
桂皮1方吋　　　　　　生粉水1湯匙
葱頭2片　　　　　　　老抽¼茶匙
葱2棵切度　　　　　　蔴油1茶匙

製法：

* 魚唇解凍後放於3杯沸水中飛水2分鐘，取出切2吋（5公分）段。放入另3杯沸水中加羌2片及酒再飛水，撈起過冷河抹乾水份。羌棄去。沸水留起候用。

* 鴨腳擦淨剪去趾甲。放入以上沸水中飛水3分鐘，取出冲淨後以老抽塗勻。隨即放入沸油中炸至金黃色，撈起過冷河隔乾水份。鑊中留下2湯匙油候用。

* 另2杯沸水放入瓦鍋中，加入各香料、羌1片及鴨腳。以中火炆1至2小時，挾起置碟中央，汁留用。

* 燒熱鑊中2湯匙油，爆香葱片。灒酒倒下鴨汁1杯，加鴨腳、魚唇及調味料。蓋上鑊蓋煮10分鐘，揭蓋以生粉水埋饋。再滴下蔴油及灒葱度即可上碟。

Ingredients:

1/2 lb (224 g) frozen fish maw
8 cups boiling water
3 slices ginger
1 tbsp wine
16 duck's webs
2 tbsp dark soy
4 cups hot oil
3 star anises
1/2 tsp xanthoxylum seeds
1 sq. in. (2.5 cm²) tangerine peel

1 sq. in. (2.5 cm²)cinnamon peel
2 sliced shallots
2 sectioned chives

Seasoning-	Gravy Mix-
1/2 tsp salt	*1 tsp cornflour*
1 tbsp sherry	*1 tbsp water*
1 tsp light soy	*1/4 tsp dark soy*
1 tsp oyster sauce	*1 tsp sesame oil*
1/2 tsp sugar	
1/8 tsp pepper	

Method:

* Defrost and blanch the fish maw in 3 cups of the boiling water for 2 minutes. Remove and cut into 2" (5 cm)sections then blanch in another 3 cups of the boiling water with 2 slices of the above ginger and the wine. Refresh and dry. Discard the ginger and keep the liquid.
* Clean and remove all the nails from the duck's webs. Blanch in the above boiling water for 3 minutes. Remove and rinse, brush with the dark soy. Deep fry in the boiling oil till golden brown. Remove, refresh and drain. Keep 2 tbsp oil for sautéeing.
* Bring the last 2 cups of water to boil in a saucepan. Put in the spices, remaining slice of ginger and the duck's webs. Simmer over moderate heat for 1 to 2 hours. Remove and keep the juice to use as stock.
* Heat the wok to bring the oil to boil. Sauté the shallots till fragrant. Sizzle the wine and pour in 1 cup of the duck juice. Return the duck's webs and fish maw into the wok with the seasoning. Cover and simmer for 10 minutes. Remove the lid and thicken the sauce with the gravy mix. Add the sesame oil and scatter the chives on top. Dish and serve.

百花油條
Stuffed Twisted Doughnuts

材料：

中蝦肉10安（280克）
粗鹽1湯匙
肥肉2安（56克）
蔥粒1湯匙
油條2條
生粉2湯匙
油4杯

調味－鹽 ½ 茶匙
　　　糖 ¼ 茶匙
　　　生粉1 茶匙
　　　胡椒粉少許
　　　蔴油1 茶匙

製法：

* 蝦挑腸以粗鹽拋勻，放水喉下沖淨用布抹乾。
* 肥肉烚熟切幼粒，蝦壓爛成茸與肥肉粒及蔥茸同置碗內，加豆粉及調味品用手撻至起膠。
* 油條切2吋度，再切開兩邊，將蝦膠釀至滿，用少許生粉抹平。
* 燒紅鑊，放入生油煮至熱時即將釀妥油條放入。再較慢火炸至金黃色，食時配喼汁或淮鹽。

Seasoning-
½ tsp salt
¼ tsp sugar
1 tsp cornflour
⅛ tsp pepper
1 tsp sesame oil

Ingredients:

10 oz (280 g) shelled shrimps
1 tbsp coarse salt
2 oz (56 g) fat pork (optional)
1 tbsp chopped chives
2 pieces twisted doughnut
2 tbsp cornflour
4 cups oil

Method:

* Devein and dredge the shrimps with the coarse salt. Wash under a running tap and dry with a clean towel.
* Blanch, refresh and finely dice the fat pork. Mash the shrimps to mix with the fat pork. Add the chopped chives and seasoning to pound until firm and springy.
* Section the doughnuts into 2" (5 cm) pieces. Cut each section in half lengthwise and dust with some cornflour then fill in the shrimp purée. Smoothen the top with a little cornflour.
* Bring the oil to boil in a wok. Slide in the stuffed doughnuts to deep fry over moderate heat until golden brown. Remove and drain. Serve with Worchestershire sauce or spicy salt.

蟹 肉 伊 麵
Crab Meat in E-Fu Noodles

材料：

伊麵 1 只 5 安（140克）
磨菇 3 隻
油 3 湯匙
銀芽 3 安（84克）
蟹肉 3 安（84克）
韮王 1 湯匙

調味—酒 1 茶匙	饍料—生粉 1 茶匙
上湯 1½ 杯	水 1 湯匙
鹽¼ 茶匙	生抽½ 茶匙
糖½ 茶匙	蔴油 1 茶匙
胡椒粉少許	
鷄粉½ 茶匙	

製法：

* 伊麵放沸水內泡過,再以凍水洗淨。
* 磨菇洗淨浸透切絲留用。
* 燒紅鑊加油 2 湯匙,煮沸,潷酒一半倒入上湯 1 杯。試妥味傾下伊麵煮 5 分鐘,以小窩盛起。
* 再燒紅鑊加入餘油煮沸,倒下銀芽爆炒片刻。潷入餘酒、上湯及調味料,再加磨菇絲煮沸,隨即傾下蟹肉兜匀,以生粉水埋饍,再滴入蔴油及洒下韮王度,淋在麵上即成。

Ingredients:

5 oz (140 g) E-Fu noodles
3 cups boiling water
3 button mushrooms
3 tbsp oil
3 oz (84 g) bean sprouts
3 oz (84 g) crab meat
1 tbsp sectioned white leeks

Seasoning-
1 tsp sherry
1½ cups stock
¼ tsp salt
½ tsp sugar
⅛ tsp pepper
½ tsp chicken powder

Gravy Mix-
1 tsp cornflour
1 tbsp water
½ tsp light soy
1 tsp sesame oil

Method:

* *Blanch the E-Fu noodles in the boiling water. Refresh and drain.*
* *Blanch and shred the mush-rooms.*
* *Heat the wok with 2 tbsp of the oil and sizzle in half of the sherry and 1 cup of the stock. Season to taste. Put in the nod-dles to simmer for 5 minutes. Remove into a bowl.*

* *Heat the other tbsp of oil in a very hot wok to sauté the bean sprouts. Sizzle in the remaining sherry, stock, seasoning and the shredded mushrooms to bring to the boil then stir in the crab meat and thicken the sauce with the cornflour mix. Drop in the sesame oil and white leeks then pour over the noodles and serve hot.*

23

星 洲 炒 米
Curried Vermicelli

材料:

米粉10安（280克）
蛋1隻
油4½湯匙
火腿4安（112克）
洋葱4安（112克）
青、紅椒各一隻
五柳料2安（56克）
韮王½安（14克）
蝦仁4安（112克）
銀芽7安（196克）

調味—咖喱醬2湯匙
　　　鹽½茶匙
　　　生抽1茶匙
　　　糖1茶匙

製法:

* 米粉用滾水浸過，隔乾水份。
* 蛋打爛用油½湯匙煎成蛋皮後切絲。
* 火腿、洋葱、青、紅椒及五柳料皆切絲。韮王洗淨切度。
* 蝦仁洗淨抹乾。燒紅鑊加油1湯匙煮沸，放入蝦仁爆炒30秒鐘盛起。
* 將鑊再燒熱用2湯匙油爆炒銀芽，盛起隔去餘油。
* 另鑊燒紅將餘油加入煮沸，放入雜菜絲及咖喱醬兜勻，加入米粉、蝦仁、火腿絲及全部材料。調妥味洒下韮王度拌勻上碟。

Ingredients:

10 oz (280 g) vermicelli
3 cups boiling water
1 egg
4½ tbsp oil
4 oz (112 g) ham
4 oz (112 g) onion
1 capsicum
1 chilli
2 oz (56 g) sweet pickles
½ oz (14 g) white leeks
4 oz (112 g) shelled shrimps
7 oz (196 g) bean sprouts

Seasoning-
2 tbsp curry paste
½ tsp salt
1 tsp light soy
1 tsp sugar

Method:

* *Soak the vermicelli in the boiling water for 20 minutes. Refresh and drain.*
* *Beat the egg and shallow fry with ½ tbsp of the oil till set. Shred.*
* *Shred the ham, onion, capsicum, chilli and pickles. Wash and section the white leeks.*
* *Clean and dry the shrimps. Heat the wok to bring 1 tbsp of the oil to boil. Sauté the shrimps for 30 seconds then remove.*
* *Reheat the wok with another 2 tbsp oil to sauté the bean sprouts for 8 seconds. Remove and drain.*

* Bring the remaining oil to boil in a heated wok. Sauté the mixed vegetables and curry till pungent. Pour in the vermicelli, shrimps, ham, pickles and the rest of the ingredients. Season to taste and mix well. Add the sectioned white leeks and dish.

肉　絲　炒　麵

Fried Noodles with Shredded Pork

材料：

炒麵餅 5 安（140克）
油 3 杯
枚肉 4 安（112克）
熟冬菇 2 隻
銀芽 6 安（168克）
葱度 1 湯匙

醃料—生抽 1 茶匙　調味—酒 1 茶匙
　　　生粉½茶匙　　　　上湯½杯
　　　糖½茶匙　　　　　鹽¼茶匙
　　　酒 1 茶匙　　　　　生抽 1 茶匙
　　　水 2 湯匙　　　　　糖 1 茶匙
　　　油 1 茶匙　　　　　胡椒粉少許
　　　　　　　　　　　　生粉水 1 湯匙
　　　　　　　　　　　　老抽¼茶匙

製法：

* 麵餅放入 3 杯沸水中飛水 1 分鐘，
  撈起過冷河隔乾水份。鑊燒熱加入
  油 1 杯煮沸，倒下麵餅炸至脆，撈
  起隔淨餘油放在長碟中剪開。
* 枚肉切絲放入醃料中醃15分鐘，冬
  菇切絲。
* 燒紅鑊，將其餘 2 杯油傾入，滑下
  肉絲泡片刻撈起隔淨餘油。鑊中留
  下油 2 湯匙候用。
* 另鑊燒熱將 2 湯匙餘油煮沸，倒入
  銀芽迅速兜勻。隨即傾下冬菇絲及
  肉絲略炒。潷酒加上湯及調味料，
  再以生粉水埋饡。最後洒上葱度拋
  勻，淋在麵上即可上桌。

Ingredients:

5 oz (140 g) noodles
3 cups boiling water
3 cups oil
4 oz (112 g) pork fillet
2 cooked Chinese mushrooms
6 oz (168 g) bean sprouts
1 tbsp sectioned spring onions

Marinade-	Seasoning-
1 tsp light soy	1 tsp wine
1/2 tsp cornflour	1/2 cup stock
1/2 tsp sugar	1/4 tsp salt
1 tsp wine	1 tsp light soy
2 tbsp water	1 tsp sugar
1 tsp oil	1/8 tsp pepper
	1 tbsp cornflour mix
	1/4 tsp dark soy

Method:

* *Blanch the noodles in the boiling water for 1 minute. Refresh and drain. Heat the wok with 1 cup of the oil to deep fry the noodles until crisp. Remove and drain off the excess oil. Place on a platter and cut into quarters with the scissors.*
* *Shred the pork fillet. Immerse in the marinade and leave for 15 minutes. Shred the mushrooms.*
* *Heat the wok and pour in the remaining 2 cups of oil. Slide in the pork to parboil for 1/2 minute. Remove and drain, leaving 2 tbsp oil for later use.*
* *Heat another clean wok to bring the 2 tbsp of oil to boil. Pour in the bean sprouts to toss for 8 seconds. Stir the shredded mushrooms and pork immediately. Sizzle the wine and pour in the stock. Add the seasoning and thicken the sauce with the cornflour mix and dark soy. Lastly scatter the spring onions and mask over the noodles. Serve hot.*

白 汁 通 粉
Macaroni in White Sauce

材料:

通粉½磅(224克)
沸水3杯
鹽2茶匙
油3湯匙
紅蘿蔔粒½杯
青紅椒各1隻,切粒
青豆4安(112克)
磨菇4隻
火腿4安(112克)
麵粉⅓杯

調味—鮮奶1杯
　　　上湯½杯
　　　鹽½茶匙
　　　胡椒粉少許
　　　糖1茶匙
　　　蔴油1茶匙

製法:

* 通粉加水及鹽煮軟,取出過冷河,隔乾水份。
* 燒紅鑊,加油煮沸,倒入通粉略炒。洒鹽、糖各少許兜勻,盛在焗兜內。
* 紅蘿蔔粒,青、紅椒粒,與青豆同置油鹽水內煨片刻,盛起候用。
* 磨菇與火腿皆切粒。
* 另鑊燒紅加入油1湯匙倒入麵粉用慢火炒勻,停火將鮮奶、上湯及調味料慢慢加入。再將全部配料傾入汁內煮至濃饈,和勻後淋在通粉上。放已預熱450度(煤氣8度)焗爐內焗20分鐘,取出熱食。

Ingredients:

1/2 lb (224 g) macaroni
3 cups boiling water
2 tsp salt
3 tbsp oil
1/2 cup diced carrot
1 green capsicum, diced
1 red capsicum, diced
4 oz (112 g) sweet peas
4 button mushrooms
4 oz (112 g) ham
1/3 cup flour

Seasoning-
1 cup milk
1/2 cup stock
1/2 tsp salt
1/8 tsp pepper
1 tsp sugar
1 tsp sesame oil

Method:

* *Cook the macaroni in the boiling water with the salt for 12 minutes. Refresh and drain. Keep the boiling salted water for later use.*
* *Heat the wok to bring 2 tbsp of the oil to boil. Stir in the macaroni to fry for 1/2 minute. Mix well and put into a baking dish.*
* *Blanch the carrot, capsicum and sweet peas in the above salted water. Refresh and drain.*
* *Dice the mushrooms and ham.*
* *Heat the wok with the last tbsp of oil. Make a roux by stirring in the flour over low heat. Turn off the heat and gradually stir in the milk, stock and seasoning.*

Return the diced ingredients into the wok to mix thoroughly in the white sauce. Pour over the macaroni and bake in a pre-heated 450°F oven (Gas Mark 8) for 20 minutes. Remove and serve hot.

29

焗 豬 扒 飯
Pork Chops with Rice

材料：

豬扒½磅（224克）
白飯3杯
蛋1只打爛
麵粉½杯
沸油3杯
紅蘿蔔4安（112克）
青豆¼杯
番茄6安（168克）
沸水2杯
洋葱4安（112克）
西芹1片

醃料—喼汁1茶匙　　　饡料—生粉1茶匙
　　　蒜頭鹽¼茶匙　　　　　水2湯匙
　　　芹菜鹽¼茶匙　　　　　老抽¼茶匙
　　　生抽½茶匙
　　　酒1茶匙
　　　糖1茶匙
　　　水2湯匙
　　　油1湯匙
調味—上湯1杯
　　　生抽1湯匙
　　　糖1茶匙
　　　胡椒粉少許

製法：

* 豬扒洗淨抹乾，以錘錘鬆，加入醃料醃15分鐘。
* 白飯與蛋同炒熟後盛在焗兜內。
* 將豬扒取出洒上麵粉少許，放熱油鍋內炸至金黃色盛起放在炒飯上面。
* 紅蘿蔔、青豆及番茄放於沸水中飛水，撈起過冷河。番茄去皮與紅蘿蔔、洋葱及西芹一同切粒。
* 各粒全部放入餘油中爆炒，倒入上湯將調味料與餘下之豬扒醃料及饡料拌勻淋在豬扒上。轉置預熱450度（煤氣8度）焗爐內焗15分鐘。熱食。

Ingredients:

1/2 lb (224 g) pork chops
3 cups cooked rice
1 beaten egg
1/2 cup flour
3 cups hot oil
4 oz (112 g) carrot
1/4 cup sweet peas

6 oz (168 g) tomatoes
2 cups boiling water
4 oz (112 g) onion
1 celery stick

Marinade-
1 tsp Worchestershire sauce
1/4 tsp garlic salt
1/4 tsp celery salt
1/2 tsp light soy
1 tsp sherry
1 tsp sugar
2 tbsp water
1 tbsp oil

Seasoning-
1 cup stock
1 tbsp light soy
1 tsp sugar
1/8 tsp pepper

Gravy Mix-
1 tsp cornflour
2 tbsp water
1/4 tsp dark soy

Method:

* Wash the pork chops then immerse in the marinade for 15 minutes. Blend in the oil and continue to marinate for 10 minutes.
* Heat the wok with 1 tbsp of the oil and stir fry the rice with the beaten egg then remove in to a baking dish.
* Dredge the pork chops in the flour to coat evenly. Put into the hot oil to deep fry until light brown. Drain on the absorbent paper. Keep 2 tbsp oil for later use. Place the pork chops on top of the rice.
* Blanch the carrot, sweet peas and tomatoes in the boiling water then refresh. Peel the tomatoes and dice with the carrot, onion and celery stick.
* Sauté the above ingredients with the oil then pour in the stock. Thicken the liquor with the mixed seasoning and gravy mix. Pour over the pork chops and bake in a preheated 450°F oven (Gas Mark 8) for 15 minutes. Serve hot.

炒 貴 刁

Rice Sticks with Assorted Meat

材料：

蝦3安（84克）
溫油2杯
枚肉3安（84克）
蛋1隻打爛
火腿1安（28克）
紅椒2隻
韮王1安（28克）
蒜頭3粒
銀芽6安（168克）
河粉10安（280克）

醃蝦料—生粉1茶匙　調味料—鹽¼茶匙
　　　　胡椒粉少許　　　　　　糖1茶匙
　　　　　　　　　　　　　　　生抽2茶匙
醃肉料—生抽1茶匙　　　　　　胡椒粉少許
　　　　生粉½茶匙　　　　　　蔴油1茶匙
　　　　酒½茶匙
　　　　糖½茶匙
　　　　水1湯匙

Ingredients:

3 oz (84 g) shrimps
2 cups warm oil
3 oz (84 g) pork fillet
1 beaten egg
1 oz (28 g) cooked ham
2 chillies
1 oz (28 g) white leeks
3 garlic cloves
6 oz (168 g) bean sprouts
10 oz (280 g) fresh rice sticks

Shrimp Marinade-
1 tsp cornflour
1/8 tsp pepper

Pork Marinade-
1 tsp light soy
1/2 tsp cornflour
1/2 tsp sugar
1/2 tsp wine
1 tbsp water

Seasoning-
1/4 tsp salt
1 tsp sugar
2 tsp light soy
1/8 tsp pepper
1 tsp sesame oil

製法：

* 蝦去殼挑腸洗净，用毛巾吸乾水份。以醃蝦料撈勻放入溫油中泡油隔净餘油。溫油攤凍候用。

* 豬肉切絲放醃肉料中醃30分鐘。轉置凍油中泡嫩油撈起隔去餘油。留起油2湯匙候用。

* 蛋液以½湯匙油煎成蛋皮後切絲。

* 火腿及紅椒切絲。韮王切度。蒜頭拍扁。

* 燒紅鑊，加入餘油煮沸放下蒜頭爆香棄去。倒下紅椒絲、銀芽炒片刻。

* 傾下河粉兜炒10秒鐘，將其餘材料及調味料加入拌勻試味，洒韮王上碟。

Method:

* *Shell, devein and wash the shrimps. Dry thoroughly with a clean towel. Coat with the shrimp marinade then parboil in the warm oil and drain. Leave the oil to cool for later use.*

* *Shred the pork then immerse in the marinade and leave for 30 minutes. Parboil in the cooled oil and drain. Keep 2 tbsp oil for later use.*

* *Shallow fry the egg into an egg sheet with 1/2 tbsp of the oil then shred.*

* *Shred the ham and chillies. Section the white leeks. Mash the garlic.*

* Heat the remaining oil in a hot wok to sauté the garlic till brown and discard. Pour in the chillies and bean sprouts to fry for a while.
* Slide in the rice sticks to toss for 10 seconds. Stir in the other ingredients and add the seasoning to toss evenly. Adjust the flavour. Scatter in the white leeks and dish.

豉 椒 牛 河

Rice Sticks with Beef and Pepper

材料:

牛柳4安 (112克)
油3杯
青紅椒各1隻
葱2棵
河粉10安 (280克)
豆豉醬2湯匙

醃料—生抽1茶匙
　　　生粉1茶匙
　　　糖½茶匙
　　　酒1茶匙
　　　水¼杯
　　　油1湯匙

調味—鹽¼茶匙
　　　酒1茶匙
　　　上湯½杯
　　　生抽1茶匙
　　　糖1½茶匙
　　　生粉水1湯匙
　　　老抽數滴

製法:

＊　牛肉切片,將醃料和勻加入醃1小時。
＊　燒紅鍋放油煮至微熱即將牛肉傾下泡嫩油,盛起留用。倒去餘油。
＊　青椒紅椒去籽切件。葱切度。
＊　鑊燒熱加油1湯匙煮沸,倒下河粉炒片刻盛在碟上。
＊　再燒紅鑊加入餘油,洒鹽爆炒青、紅椒及豆豉醬。潵酒加上湯及調味料拌勻,傾下牛肉片撈勻淋在河粉上即成。

Ingredients:

4 oz (112 g) beef fillet
3 cups oil
1 green capsicum
1 chilli
2 chives
10 oz (280 g) rice sticks
2 tbsp preserved black bean paste

Marinade-	*Gravy Mix-*
1 tsp light soy	*1 tsp cornflour*
1 tsp cornflour	*1 tbsp water*
½ tsp sugar	*½ tsp dark soy*
1 tsp wine	
¼ cup water	
1 tbsp oil	

Seasoning-
¼ tsp salt
1 tsp wine
½ cup stock
1 tsp light soy
1½ tsp sugar

Method:

* *Slice the beef and immerse in the marinade to stand for an hour.*
* *Pour the oil into a heated wok. Quickly slide in the marinated beef to parboil in the warm oil for 20 seconds. Remove and drain. Retain 3 tbsp of oil for later use.*
* *Deseed and cut the capsicum and chilli. Section the chives.*
* *Heat the wok with 1 tbsp of the oil to put in the rice sticks. Toss evenly and dish.*
* *Reheat the wok with the remaining oil and sprinkle in the salt to sauté the capsicum and chilli with the black bean paste. Sizzle*

the wine and pour in the stock
and seasoning. Thicken the
sauce with the gravy mix. Return
the beef into the wok to mix well
with the gravy. Pour over the
rice sticks and serve hot.

义　烧　飯

Rice with Roast Pork

材料：

枚肉10安（280克）
白飯 4 杯

醃肉料—柱候醬 2 茶匙
　　　　海鮮醬 2 茶匙
　　　　蔴醬 1 茶匙
　　　　玫瑰露 1 茶匙
　　　　葱頭 1 粒
　　　　蒜頭 1 粒
　　　　生抽⅓杯
　　　　糖¼杯

塗面——蜜糖 3 湯匙
　　　　蔴油 1 茶匙

製法：

* 枚肉洗淨切長條，用刀鎅礦石紋。
* 上列各調味料和勻，將枚肉放入醃50分鐘。
* 醃好之枚肉放入已預開450度之焗爐內焗15分鐘。取出塗上蜜糖，重放爐中再焗10分鐘。取出攤凍切片，塗以蔴油。
* 熱白飯4杯分放3個深碟中，將叉燒排在上面，醃叉燒料可煮沸淋少許在飯上。用生抽熱油淋上亦可，最後洒上蔴油。

Ingredients:

10 oz (280 g) pork fillet
4 bowls hot cooked rice

Pork Marinade-
2 tsp ground bean paste
2 tsp Hoi Sin paste
1 tsp peanut butter
1 tsp sherry
1 shallot
1 garlic clove
⅓ cup light soy
¼ cup sugar

Coating-
3 tbsp honey
1 tsp sesame oil

Method:

* Wash the pork fillet, trim and cut into 2 thick strips. Score some criss-cross patterns on the surface of the meat with a sharp knife.
* Mix the above marinade evenly and immerse the meat to stand for 50 minutes. Save the marinade for later use as sauce.
* Preheat the oven to 450°F (Gas Mark 6). Put in the meat to roast for 15 minutes. Brush with the honey. Turn and continue to roast for another 10 minutes. Remove and slice when cool.
* Divide the rice amongst 3 platters. Arrange the sliced pork on top. Heat the sauce and spoon over the rice. Sprinkle with the sesame oil and serve hot.

蠔 油 鮑 片
Abalone in Oyster Sauce

材料:

罐鮑1罐
西生菜1個
羌2片
葱頭1粒
油2湯匙

調味—紹酒1茶匙　饡料—生粉1茶匙
　　　鮑魚水⅔杯　　　　水1湯匙
　　　蠔油3湯匙　　　　胡椒粉少許
　　　糖1茶匙　　　　　老抽¼茶匙
　　　　　　　　　　　蔴油½茶匙

製法:

* 鮑魚開後隔去水份,以利刀片成大
  薄片。
* 生菜洗淨,置已放油鹽之沸水中煨
  片刻,撈起隔去水份。
* 羌切絲,葱頭去衣切片。
* 玻璃兜一個,將生菜放入排好。
* 燒紅鑊加油爆香羌葱片。濺酒加入
  鮑魚水煮沸。試妥味後以生粉水埋
  饡。隨即傾下鮑魚和勻倒在生菜上
  即成。

Gravy Mix-
1 tsp cornflour
1 tbsp water
1/8 tsp pepper
1/4 tsp dark soy
1/2 tsp sesame oil

Ingredients:

1 tin abalone
1 head of lettuce
2 cups boiling salted water
4 tbsp oil
2 slices ginger
1 shallot

Seasoning-
1 tsp sherry
2/3 cup abalone juice
3 tbsp oyster sauce
1 tsp sugar

Method:

* Slice the abalone into thin pieces.
* Wash and trim the lettuce. Blanch in the boiling salted water with 2 tbsp of the oil for a few seconds. Drain and leave aside. Arrange the cooked lettuce in a deep platter.
* Shred the ginger. Peel and slice the shallot.

* Heat the wok with the remaining oil to sauté the ginger and shallot. Sizzle the sherry and pour in the juice to bring to the boil. Adjust the flavor to taste then thicken the sauce with the gravy mix. Slide in the abalone to mix well and scoop over the lettuce. Serve hot.

炸　生　蠔
Deep Fried Oysters

材料：

生蠔1磅（½公斤）
鹽2湯匙
生粉3湯匙
油2湯匙
羗片1安（28克）
葱度1安（28克）
酒3湯匙
水3杯
沸油4杯

調味—羗汁1湯匙　　脆漿—麵粉1杯
　　　幼鹽½茶匙　　　　　生粉2茶匙
　　　糖1茶匙　　　　　　發粉2茶匙
　　　胡椒粉少許　　　　　水½杯
　　　蔴油1茶匙　　　　　豬油3湯匙
　　　　　　　　　　　　　鹽½茶匙

製法：

* 生蠔用鹽及生粉2湯匙洗淨，再以清水過清隔去水份。
* 鑊燒紅加油,煮沸爆香羗片及葱度,潛酒加水再煮沸。將生蠔傾下一滾,即以罩籬盛起,再用乾毛巾吸乾水份。調味料和勻將生蠔放入醃20分鐘。
* 麵粉、生粉及發粉同篩入碗內。慢慢注入水拌勻,再加入油及鹽和成粉漿。
* 生蠔用剩下之生粉塗妥放入粉漿中捲勻。
* 炸油煮至僅沸時,把生蠔逐隻放入炸至金黃色,撈起吸淨油上碟。與淮鹽、喼汁同食。

Ingredients:

1 lb (¹/₂ kg) oysters
2 tbsp salt
3 tbsp cornflour
2 tbsp oil
1 oz (28 g) sliced ginger
1 oz (28 g) sectioned chives
3 tbsp sherry
3 cups water
4 cups hot oil

Seasoning-
1 tbsp ginger juice
¹/₂ tsp salt
1 tsp sugar
¹/₈ tsp pepper
1 tsp sesame oil

Batter-
1 cup flour
2 tsp cornflour
2 tsp baking powder
¹/₂ cup water
3 tbsp oil
¹/₂ tsp salt

Method:

* *Clean the oysters with the salt and 2 tbsp of the cornflour. Wash thoroughly and drain.*
* *Bring the oil to boil in a hot wok. Sauté the ginger and chives then sizzle the sherry and add the water to bring to boil. Scald the oysters and remove immediately. Drain and dry with a towel. Marinate with the seasoning for 20 minutes.*
* *Sift the flour, cornflour and the baking powder into a mixing*

bowl. Stir in the water slowly to bind well. Add the oil and salt to blend into a smooth batter.
* Dust each oyster with the remaining tbsp of the cornflour then toss in the batter to coat evenly.

* Bring the oil to boil over moderate heat. Slide in the oysters one by one to deep fry until golden brown. Remove and dish. Serve with Worchestershire sauce and spicy salt.

41

菊花鱸魚球
Fish Ball with Chrysanthemum

材料：

鱸魚肉10安（280克）
胡椒粉¼茶匙　　調味—鹽¼茶匙
生粉1茶匙　　　　酒1茶匙
白菊花1朵　　　　上湯¼杯
西芹數片　　　　生抽2茶匙
紅蘿蔔數片　　　糖1茶匙
沸鹽水1杯　　　生粉水1湯匙
羌2片　　　　　麻油½茶匙
葱頭1粒
蒜頭1粒
油4杯
葱3棵切度

製法：

* 鱸魚以水略洗後用布吸乾水份，切成骨牌型，用胡椒粉加生粉塗勻。
* 菊花洗淨剪起花瓣留用，其餘棄去。
* 西芹、紅蘿蔔洗淨切妥一同放入沸鹽水中飛水。撈起隔去水份。羌及葱、蒜頭拍扁。
* 燒紅鑊加油煮至微熱即將魚塊倒入泡油。取出隔淨餘油，留下油2湯匙在鑊中候用。
* 再燒熱鑊洒鹽爆香羌、葱、蒜棄去。倒下西芹、紅蘿蔔及魚塊兜勻。潷酒加上湯及調味料，試妥味後以生粉水埋饡。最後洒上菊花、葱度及麻油即可上碟。

Ingredients:

10 oz (280 g) fish fillet
1/4 tsp pepper
1 tsp cornflour
1 white chrysanthemum
few celery sticks
few slices carrot
1 cup boiling salted water
2 pieces ginger
1 shallot
1 garlic clove
4 cups oil
3 sectioned chives

Seasoning-
1/4 tsp salt
1 tsp sherry
1/4 cup stock
2 tsp light soy
1 tsp sugar

Gravy Mix-
1/2 tsp cornflour
1/2 tbsp water
1/2 tsp sesame oil

Method:

* Wash and dry the fish. Cut into thick rectangular pieces then dredge evenly in the pepper and cornflour.
* Wash the chrysanthemum, remove the petals and leave aside.
* Wash, cut and blanch the celery and carrot in the boiling salted water. Remove and drain. Mash the ginger, shallot and garlic.
* Heat the wok to bring the oil to just boil then parboil the fish for a while. Remove and drain, leaving 2 tbsp oil in the wok.
* Reheat the wok with the oil and sprinkle in the salt to sauté the ginger, shallot and garlic till aromatic then discard. Stir in the celery, carrot and fish to mix well. Sizzle the sherry, add the stock and season to taste. Thicken the sauce with the gravy mix. Scatter the chrysanthemum petals, sectioned chives and sesame oil to mix well. Dish and serve hot.

43

炸 鳳 尾 蝦
Prawn Cutlets

材料：

大蝦20只　　　　蘸料—沙律醬½杯
麵粉½杯　　　　　茄汁½杯
鹽½茶匙
胡椒粉少許
蛋3隻打爛
麵包糠1杯
炸油½鍋
西洋菜數棵

製法：

* 蝦洗淨去頭及壳，保留尾部挑去腸臟後用鹽稍洗。
* 用毛巾吸乾水份後，把刀在蝦背輕剖一刀擺平。
* 麵粉、胡椒粉與鹽同篩在碟上，將蝦放在粉內一拖。
* 雞蛋打勻，將蝦逐只放入沾滿蛋液跟着轉放入麵包糠中打滾。
* 燒紅鑊注入油半鍋煮至微沸時即將蝦投入炸至金黃色上碟。
* 西洋菜洗淨摘妥放在碟中央點綴。沙律醬及茄汁跟上。

Ingredients:

20 prawns
½ cup flour
½ tsp salt
⅛ tsp pepper
3 beaten eggs
1 cup breadcrumbs
½ wok oil for deep frying
1 oz (28 g) water cress

Dipping-
½ cup mayonnaise
½ cup tomato ketchup

Method:

* Shell ¾ of each prawn, leaving the tail end intact. Devein, wash then dry with a towel.
* Slit the back of the prawns, open up and press lightly to flatten.
* Sift the flour, salt and pepper on a platter to coat the prawns evenly. Dip the prawns in the beaten eggs then roll in the breadcrumbs to cover evenly.
* Gently bring the oil to boil in a hot wok. Slide in the prawns to deep fry until golden brown. Drain and dish.
* Garnish with the water cress and serve with the mayonnaise and tomato ketchup.

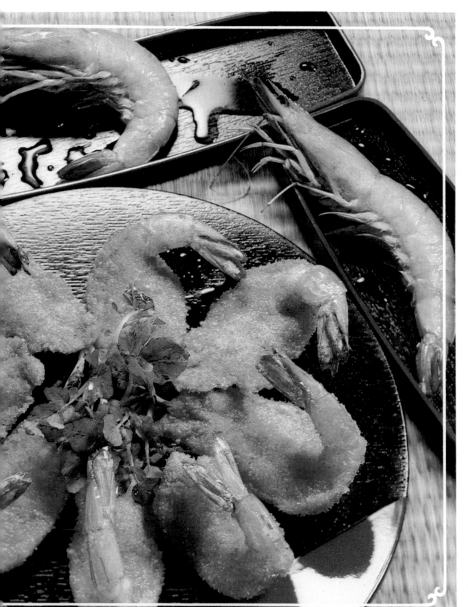

四川大蝦
Szechuen Prawns

材料：

大蝦 1 磅（½公斤）
鹽 ½ 茶匙
紅椒 2 只
青葱數條
芫茜 2 棵
葱頭 2 粒
蒜頭 1 粒
薑 3 片
油 4 湯匙

調味─豆瓣醬 1 湯匙
　　　紹酒 1 湯匙
　　　水 2 湯匙
　　　茄汁 1 湯匙
　　　生抽 2 茶匙
　　　糖 2 茶匙
　　　生粉水 1 茶匙
　　　蔴油 1 茶匙

製法：

* 大蝦從背上挑去腸臟，剪去爪子，以粗鹽洒在上面，放水喉下冲洗乾淨。
* 紅椒切開去籽，然後切絲或切粒，留用。
* 葱切度，芫茜摘葉，葱頭、蒜頭薑切絲。
* 燒紅鑊，加油。油熱時，將蝦平放在鑊中，頭向鑊內，以中火煎約 3 分鐘。反轉再煎 2 分鐘，灒酒少許，即盛起。
* 另鑊燒紅，加油煮滾，投入葱蒜頭炸香。加薑片紅椒絲及豆瓣醬兜炒片刻，灒酒加上湯少許，然後加茄汁調味。以豆粉水開健慢慢煮至濃度適合時，即加葱度及已煎之蝦，再加油少許快手兜勻上碟。以芫茜點綴。

Ingredients:

1 lb (½ kg) prawns
½ tsp salt
2 red chillies
3 chives
2 parsley sprigs
2 shallots
1 garlic clove
3 slices ginger
4 tbsp oil

Seasoning-
1 tbsp hot broad bean paste
1 tbsp sherry
2 tbsp water
1 tbsp tomato ketchup
2 tsp light soy
2 tsp sugar
1 tsp cornflour mix
1 tsp sesame oil

Method:

* Wash, trim and devein the prawns. Dry and sprinkle the above salt on to each prawn.
* Deseed and shred the chillies. Leave aside for later use.
* Section the chives. Wash and trim the parsley. Shred the shallots, garlic and ginger.
* Heat the wok to bring 2 tbsp of the oil to boil. Place the prawns into the wok with the head pointing towards the centre. Shallow fry over medium heat for 3 minutes. Turn over and fry for another 2 minutes then remove.
* Clean and reheat the wok to bring the remaining oil to boil. Sauté the shallots, garlic, ginger

46

and chillies till pungent. Stir in
the broad bean paste and return
the prawns into the wok. Sizzle
the sherry and add the seasoning
to toss evenly. Blend in the
cornflour mix then garnish with
the parsley and chives and dish.

雞錦豆腐羹
Bean Curd Chop Suey Chowder

材料：

板豆腐½磅（224克）
雞肝1隻
蝦仁1安（28克）
草菰1安（28克）
紅蘿蔔1安（28克）
韮王2棵
酒1茶匙
羌汁1茶匙
生粉½茶匙
胡椒粉少許
青豆1安（28克）
油2湯匙

調味一酒1茶匙
　　　水4杯
　　　鹽2茶匙
　　　雞精1粒
　　　糖½茶匙
　　　胡椒粉少許
　　　生粉水3湯匙
　　　老抽½茶匙
　　　蔴油1茶匙

製法：

* 全部材料皆切粒。
* 雞肝以酒及羌汁醃片刻。
* 蝦仁洗淨抹乾，用生粉及胡椒粉撈勻。
* 蝦仁及全部粒（韮王除外）一同放入沸水中飛水。撈起過冷河隔乾水份。
* 燒紅鑊加油，潷酒傾入水煮沸。倒下調味料及全部配料煮2分鐘。以生粉水及老抽埋饂，再滴入蔴油拌勻後用湯兜盛起。最後洒下韮王即成。

Ingredients:

1/2 lb (224 g) bean curd
1 chicken liver
1 oz (28 g) shelled shrimps
1 oz (28 g) straw mushrooms
1 oz (28 g) carrot
2 chives or white leeks
1 tsp wine
1 tsp ginger juice
1/2 tsp cornflour
1/8 tsp pepper
1 oz (28 g) sweet peas
3 cups boiling water
2 tbsp oil

Seasoning-
1 tsp sherry
4 cups water
2 tsp salt
1 chicken cube
1/2 tsp sugar
1/8 tsp pepper
3 tbsp cornflour mix
1/2 tsp dark soy
1 tsp sesame oil

Method:

* Dice all the ingredients.
* Marinate the chicken liver with the wine and ginger juice.
* Clean, dry and coat the shrimps with the cornflour and pepper.
* Blanch the shrimps and all the diced ingredients, except the chives, in the boiling water. Refresh and drain.
* Bring the oil to boil in a heated saucepan. Sizzle the sherry and

pour in the water to bring to boil. Stir in the seasoning and all the ingredients to simmer for 2 minutes. Thicken the soup with the cornflour mix and dark soy. Drop in the sesame oil to mix well. Scoop into a serving bowl then scatter the chives on top.

蓬萊幻影
Coconut Consomme

材料：

冬菇2安（56克）
椰子2個
沸水4杯
羗2片

調味一鹽2茶匙
　　　糖1茶匙
　　　油1湯匙
　　　酒½茶匙

製法：

* 花菇洗淨浸透，剪去菇蒂。用一半鹽及糖加油同撈勻留用
* 椰子用鋸鋸開頂部，倒去椰水。每個椰子注入2杯沸水，將椰蓋蓋上。置蒸籠內燉1小時。
* 椰子燉好後，揭開倒入醃妥之冬菇、羗片及酒，再蓋上蓋續燉20分鐘。取出試妥味即可飲用。

Ingredients:

2 oz (56 g) Chinese mushrooms
2 coconuts
4 cups boiling water
2 slices ginger

Seasoning-
2 tsp salt
1 tsp sugar
1 tbsp oil
$1/2$ tsp sherry

Method:

* Wash and soak the mushrooms. Remove the stalks and marinate with half of the above salt, sugar and all the oil.
* Saw off the tops of the coconuts. Discard the juice and fill each coconut with 2 cups of water. Recover the coconuts and cook in a steamer over a wok of boiling water for an hour.
* Remove the lid and pour in the marinated mushrooms, ginger and sherry. Continue to steam for 20 minutes. Season to taste and serve hot.

生菜雙丸湯
Double Meatball Soup

材料：

蝦1磅（½公斤）
鹽1湯匙
枚肉6安（168克）
馬蹄4粒
生菜1棵
油2湯匙
水5杯

醃蝦料—蛋白½隻
　　　　鹽½茶匙
　　　　胡椒粉少許

醃肉料—生抽2茶匙
　　　　糖1茶匙
　　　　生粉1茶匙
　　　　水2湯匙
　　　　油1湯匙

調味料—酒1茶匙
　　　　鹽2茶匙
　　　　雞粉½茶匙
　　　　胡椒粉少許

製法：

* 蝦去殼用鹽冲洗乾淨，以毛巾吸乾水份及吹乾。

* 蝦肉壓爛放於深盆內，加入醃蝦料和勻，用力撻至起膠後雪1小時。取出以手擠成小丸子。

* 枚肉與馬蹄洗淨磨爛成茸，放入醃肉料中醃30分鐘後，用手撻至起膠。亦以手擠成與蝦丸同樣大小。生菜洗淨。

* 燒紅鑊加油，潰酒加水煮沸，將肉丸、蝦丸及生菜放入煮3分鐘。試妥味後轉盛湯窩中上桌。

Ingredients:

1 lb (¹/₂ kg) shrimps
1 tbsp salt
6 oz (168 g) pork fillet
4 water chestnuts
1 lettuce
2 tbsp oil
5 cups boiling water

Shrimp Marinade-
¹/₂ egg white
¹/₂ tsp salt
¹/₈ tsp pepper

Pork Marinade- Seasoning-
2 tsp light soy   1 tsp wine
1 tsp sugar   2 tsp salt
1 tsp cornflour   ¹/₂ tsp chicken powder
2 tbsp water   ¹/₈ tsp pepper
1 tbsp oil

Method:

* Shell and toss the shrimps in the salt. Rinse under a running tap then dry with a towel.
* Mash the shrimps and add the marinade to mix well then pound until firm. Chill for an hour then shape into small balls.
* Clean and mince the pork and water chestnuts. Immerse in the pork marinade to stand for 30 minutes. Pound until springy. Shape into small balls the same size as the shrimpballs. Wash the lettuce.
* Heat the oil in a hot wok and sizzle in the wine. Pour in the water and add the meatballs, shrimpballs and lettuce to simmer for 3 minutes. Season to taste then serve in the soup bowls.

瑤　柱　羹
Dried Scallop Chowder

材料：

瑤柱2安（56克）
沸水1½杯
魷魚2安（56克）
熟冬菇2安（56克）
火腿2安（56克）
紅蘿蔔2安（56克）
笋2安（56克）
韮王¼安（7克）
油2湯匙
水4杯＋瑤柱水1杯
鷄蛋1只

調味－酒1茶匙
　　　鹽1茶匙
　　　糖⅔茶匙
　　　胡椒粉少許
　　　生粉水2湯匙
　　　老抽½茶匙

製法：

* 瑤柱用沸水浸1小時後撕開蒸30分鐘，瑤柱水留起候用。
* 全部材料洗淨切絲。韮王切度。
* 鍋燒紅加油，濽酒傾入水及瑤柱絲、魷魚絲、冬菇絲及紅蘿蔔絲煮10分鐘，隨即將其餘材料加入續煮5分鐘。調妥味。
* 生粉水慢慢流入湯中搞勻。最後拌入鷄蛋及韮王和勻傾入湯碗內。

Ingredients:

2 oz (56 g) dried scallops
1½ cup boiling water
2 oz (56 g) fresh squid
2 oz (56 g) cooked Chinese mushrooms
2 oz (56 g) ham
2 oz (56 g) carrot
2 oz (56 g) bamboo shoot (optional)
¼ oz (7 g) white leeks
2 tbsp oil
4 cups water + 1 cup scallop water
1 beaten egg

Seasoning-
1 tsp sherry
1 tsp salt
⅔ tsp sugar
⅛ tsp pepper
2 tbsp cornflour mix
½ tsp dark soy

Method:

* *Soak the scallops in the boiling water for an hour. Tear into fine shreds and steam for 30 minutes. Keep the scallop water for later use.*
* *Clean and shred all the other ingredients. Section the leeks.*
* *Heat the saucepan with the oil. Sizzle in the sherry then add the water to bring to the boil. Pour in the scallops, squid, mushrooms and carrot to simmer for 10 minutes. Stir in the remaining ingredients to simmer for another 5 minutes. Season to taste.*

* Slowly blend in the cornflour
  mix to thicken. Finally trickle in
  the beaten egg and sprinkle in
  the   white   leeks.   Serve
  immediately in soup bowls.

酸　辣　湯
Hot and Sour Soup

材料：

木耳½安（14克）
沸水2杯
豆腐2件
火腿2安（56克）
魷魚2安（56克）
熟冬菇4隻
紅蘿蔔3安（86克）
油2湯匙
蛋1隻打爛
麻油1茶匙

胡椒粉¼茶匙
葱絲½湯匙

調味—酒1茶匙
水4杯
鹽1½茶匙
生抽1茶匙
糖1茶匙
醋3湯匙
辣油1茶匙
生粉水2湯匙

製法：

* 木耳浸於沸水中約1小時，取出剪去硬蒂洗淨切絲，飛水沖凍留用。
* 全部材料洗淨切絲。
* 鍋燒熱加油，讚酒加入水煮沸。倒下上述各絲煮10分鐘，試妥味。
* 生粉水與蛋液搞勻拌入。
* 麻油及胡椒粉洒入湯窩內，即將湯傾入窩中。洒下葱絲即可上桌。

Ingredients:

1/2 oz (14 g) black fungus
2 cups hot water
2 pieces bean curd
2 oz (56 g) ham
2 oz (56 g) squid
4 cooked Chinese mushrooms
3 oz (84 g) carrot
2 tbsp oil
1 beaten egg
1 tsp sesame oil
1/4 tsp pepper
1/2 tbsp shredded chives

Seasoning-
1 tsp sherry	3 tbsp white vinegar
4 cups water	1 tsp hot sauce
1 1/2 tsp salt	2 tbsp cornflour mix
1 tsp light soy	
1 tsp sugar	

Method:

* Soak the fungus in the hot water for an hour. Trim, shred, blanch and refresh.
* Clean and shred all the other ingredients.
* Heat the saucepan with the oil. Sizzle the sherry and pour in the water to bring to boil. Put in all the ingredients and simmer for 10 minutes. Season to taste.
* Stir in the cornflour mix and trickle in the beaten egg.
* Drop the sesame oil and pepper into a soup bowl. Pour in the soup and sprinkle the chives on top. Serve hot.

豬　　脚　　凍
Diced Trotter in Aspic

材料：	**Ingredients:**

豬手1只
鷄湯5杯
丁香6粒
八角6粒
羌2片
大菜½安（14克）
水2杯

調味一鹽2茶匙
　　　糖1茶匙
　　　酒1茶匙
　　　老抽1茶匙
　　　蔴油1茶匙
　　　胡椒粉少許

1 pig's trotter
5 cups chicken broth
6 cloves
6 star anises
2 slices ginger
1/2 oz (14 g) agar agar
2 cups water

製法：

* 豬手用火燒淨毛放沸水中洗淨，用毛巾抹乾水份。

* 鍋內放入鷄湯、丁香、八角及羌片煮10分鐘。將豬手原隻放入煲至離骨。取出豬手攤凍去骨切丁。棄去香料。鷄湯留起候用。

* 大菜放水中浸至軟，撈起揸乾水份後放入鷄湯內加豬手粒煮20分鐘。試妥味倒在玻璃長盆或咖喱模中攤凍。置雪柜內雪硬，切片而食。

Seasoning-
2 tsp salt
1 tsp sugar
1 tsp sherry
1 tsp dark soy
1 tsp sesame oil
1/8 tsp pepper

Method:

* Singe and wash the trotter in the boiling water. Dry with a clean towel.
* Bring the broth to boil with the cloves, star anises and ginger for 10 minutes. Add the trotter to simmer until soft. Remove and discard the spices. Leave the trotter to cool then debone and dice. Keep the broth for later use.
* Soak the agar agar in the water until soft. Squeeze out the excess water then place in the saucepan with the spiced broth and diced trotter to simmer for 20 minutes. Season to taste. Remove into an oblong container or jelly mould and leave to cool. Chill in the refrigerator until set. Slice and serve cold.

烧　　肉
Roast Belly Pork

材料：

五花肉1塊重2磅（1公斤）
粗鹽2湯匙
幼鹽1湯匙
檸檬½隻

調味—香鹽2湯匙
　　　糖1茶匙
　　　胡椒粉少許

製法：

* 五花肉燒淨毛用粗鹽擦去皮上脂肪
  。清洗乾淨隔去水份。
* 鑊中放入井字蒸架，注入清水至高
  於蒸架½吋（1.3公分）然後將水煮
  沸。
* 五花肉皮向下放置蒸架上。沸水必
  須剛浸到豬皮。以中火煮約半小時
  （不要覆蓋）至豬皮軟。
* 取出五花肉皮向下放在砧板上以利
  刀每隔1吋（2.5公分）鎅1刀。將
  調味料和勻擦在肉上及縫中。
* 反轉五花肉以叉在皮上刺上無數小
  洞，用幼鹽擦在皮上，再洒檸汁擦
  勻。放置一旁吊乾約4至5小時。
* 將五花肉放入已預熱375度（煤氣
  5度）之焗爐內燒15分鐘。轉以猛
  火500度（煤氣9度）續燒20至30
  分鐘至皮完全起泡即可取出斬件。

Ingredients:

2 lb (1 kg) belly pork
2 tbsp coarse salt
1 tbsp fine salt
¹/₂ lemon

Seasoning-
2 tbsp spicy salt
1 tsp sugar
¹/₈ tsp pepper

Method:

* *Singe and scrape the pork skin
  then rub with the coarse salt till
  greaseless. Wash and drain.*
* *Place a steaming rack in a wok.
  Pour enough water to cover the
  rack so that the water only
  touches the skin of the pork
  when it is put on the rack. Bring
  the water to boil.*
* *Place the belly pork on the rack
  with the skin side facing down.
  Cook over moderate heat, unco-
  vered, for 30 minutes until the
  pork skin softens.*
* *Slash a few cuts at 1" (2.5 cm)
  intervals on the meat then rub in
  the mixed seasoning.*
* *Use a fork to pierce lightly all
  over the skin. Rub first with the
  fine salt then the lemon. Tie the
  pork with 2 pieces of wire to
  make the skin bulge out. Leave
  aside to dry for 4 to 5 hours.*
* *Place the pork in a preheated
  375°F (Gas Mark 5) oven to
  roast for 15 minutes. Increase
  the temperature to 500°F (Gas
  Mark 9) when bubbles begin to
  appear on the rind. Continue to
  roast for another 20 to 30
  minutes until the skin is crisp
  and the meat thoroughly
  cooked.*

燒 排 骨
Roast Spare Ribs

材料：

肉排2磅（1公斤）
蜜糖½杯塗面用

調味－磨豉1安（28克）
　　海鮮醬1安（28克）
　　蔴醬½安（14克）
　　沙糖3安（84克）
　　生抽3安（84克）
　　香鹽1茶匙
　　蔴油1茶匙
　　蒜茸2顆
　　乾葱2顆
　　玫瑰露½安（14克）
　　花紅粉少許

製法：

* 肉排原件洗淨，吊乾略鋝。
* 上述調味品拌勻，將糖攪溶。
* 把已鋝好之肉排放入以上拌勻調味料中醃1小時。取出放在焗盆中之塗油鐵架上。
* 焗爐預先開定450度（煤氣8度），將肉排放入焗15分鐘。取出塗上蜜糖，放回爐內再焗15分鐘後，取出塗第二次蜜糖。重放回爐內續焗6分鐘。取出斬件上碟。

Ingredients:

2 lb (1 kg) spare ribs
1/2 cup honey for coating

Seasoning-
1 oz (28 g) ground bean paste
1 oz (28 g) Hoi Sin paste
1/2 oz (14 g) sesame paste
3 oz (84 g) sugar
3 oz (84 g) light soy
1 tsp spicy salt
1 tsp sesame oil
2 mashed garlic
2 mashed shallots
1/2 oz (14 g) sherry or Chinese rose
　wine
1 tsp red food colouring

Method:

* Wash the whole cut of spare ribs and dry with a towel. Score some criss-cross pattern on the meat.
* Place all the seasoning in a bowl and mix thoroughly.
* Immerse the ribs in the mixed seasoning and leave to stand for an hour. Remove on to a greased baking rack.
* Bake in a preheated 450°F oven (Gas Mark 8) for 15 minutes. Brush all over with the honey then return into the oven to bake for another 15 minutes. Coat with the honey again and bake for a final 6 minutes. Remove and chop into serving pieces.

金華玉樹鷄

Boneless Chicken with Ham

Ingredients:

1 chicken, about 3 lb (1½ kg)
1 tbsp coarse salt
3 slices ginger
3 chives
2 star anises
6 oz (168 g) Virginia ham
3 cups boiling water
10 oz (280 g) green vegetables
2 tbsp oil
2 shallots

材料：

光鷄一隻，重3磅（1½公斤）
粗鹽1湯匙
羌3片
葱3條
八角2粒
火腿6安（168克）
沸水3杯
菜薳10安（280克）
油2湯匙
葱頭2粒

調味—鹽2茶匙
　　　酒2茶匙
　　　上湯⅔杯
　　　生抽1茶匙
　　　糖½茶匙
　　　胡椒粉少許
　　　生粉水1湯匙
　　　蔴油1茶匙

製法：

* 　光鷄用粗鹽擦淨鷄皮，冲洗乾淨，
　　以毛巾吸乾水份。
* 　鷄皮用鹽及酒各1茶匙塗勻。鷄肚
　　以另一半鹽及酒、羌片、葱及八角
　　塞入搖勻。放蒸籠內猛火蒸20分鐘
　　。停火取出攤凍去骨切成骨牌片。
* 　火腿放入沸水中飛水，過冷河隔乾
　　水份。沸水留起候用。火腿亦切成
　　骨牌片，然後將鷄與火腿梅花間竹
　　地排在長碟上。
* 　菜薳用留下沸水飛水，隔去水份，
　　排在碟邊。
* 　燒紅鑊加油煮沸爆香葱頭後棄去，
　　傾下上湯加調味料試妥味，以生粉
　　水流入和成稀饙，淋上鷄肉上即可
　　上桌。

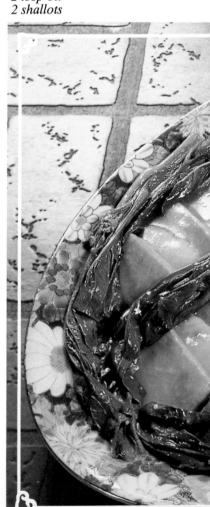

Seasoning-
2 tsp salt   1/2 tsp sugar
2 tsp sherry   1/8 tsp pepper
2/3 cup stock   1 tbsp cornflour mix
1 tsp light soy   1 tsp sesame oil

Method:

* Clean the chicken skin by rubbing with the salt. Refresh and dry with a towel.
* Rub 1 tsp each of the salt and sherry over the chicken skin. Place another tsp of salt and sherry, the ginger, chives and star anises inside the chicken. Steam over high heat for 20 minutes then remove and leave to cool. Debone and cut the chicken into bite-sized pieces.
* Blanch the ham in the boiling water. Refresh and drain. Keep the water for later use. Cut the ham into similar size as the chicken. Arrange the ham and chicken slices alternatively on an oval platter.
* Blanch the green vegetables in the above boiling water. Drain and arrange round the chicken and ham.
* Heat the oil in a hot wok to sauté the shallots then discard. Pour in the stock and season to taste. Thicken the sauce with the cornflour mix. Pour evenly over the dish and serve hot.

65

蔴辣鷄件

Chicken in Hot Sesame Paste

Ingredients:

10 oz (280 g) boneless chicken
1 tbsp sesame paste
1 tbsp hot mustard
1 beaten egg
1 cup cornflour
4 cups oil
1 parsley sprig

材料：

鷄肉10安（280克）
蔴醬1湯匙
芥醬1湯匙
蛋1隻打爛
生粉1杯
油4杯
番茜1棵

調味—羗汁2茶匙
酒1茶匙
生抽1茶匙
生粉1茶匙
鹽¼茶匙
糖1茶匙
胡椒粉少許

製法：

* 鷄肉切片加蔴醬、芥醬及全部調味料撈勻醃30分鐘。
* 鷄蛋放入鷄件中拌勻，隔去醃料，再上乾生粉。
* 燒紅鑊注入油煮沸，將鷄件投入炸約4分鐘至金黃色。盛起攤凍。
* 攤凍後再炸1分鐘，隔去餘油，切成小件，排放在碟上。以紅蘿蔔花及番茜裝飾。喼汁、淮鹽跟上。

Seasoning-
2 tsp ginger juice
1 tsp sherry
1 tsp light soy
1 tsp cornflour
1/4 tsp salt
1 tsp sugar
1/8 tsp pepper

Method:

* *Slice and marinate the chicken with the sesame paste, mustard and all the seasoning for 30 minutes.*
* *Stir in the beaten egg to mix well.*

Remove the excess marinade then coat evenly with the cornflour.
* *Bring the oil to boil in a very hot wok. Deep fry the chicken for approximately 4 minutes or until golden brown. Drain and leave to cool.*
* *Deep fry the chicken again for another minute then drain on absorbent paper. Cut into smaller pieces and dish. Garnish with carrot flower and the parsley. Serve with Worchestershire sauce and spicy salt.*

67

咖喱鷄
Curried Chicken

材料：

香茅1支
大洋葱2個
油5湯匙
咖喱粉3湯匙
黃羌粉1茶匙
羌2片
蒜頭3粒
馬拉贊2茶匙
紅椒4隻
鷄1隻約3磅（1½公斤）
羌汁2湯匙
酒2湯匙
去皮熟薯仔1磅（½公斤）
水1杯
椰汁2杯

調味—鹽1茶匙
　　　糖1湯匙
　　　鷄粉½茶匙

製法：

* 香茅洗淨斬去頭尾棄去，只用中央約4吋（10公分）長，拍扁候用。洋葱略刷，放搥坎中搥成泥。
* 用油2湯匙將一半咖喱粉及黃羌粉攪成濃漿。然後再以油1湯匙爆香洋葱及咖喱漿。
* 將香茅、羌片、蒜頭、馬拉贊及紅椒一同搥至成滑漿，再與咖喱漿拌勻。
* 鷄洗淨斬件，用羌汁、酒及其餘咖喱粉和勻醃1小時。
* 燒紅鑊加入餘油，倒入混合之材料轉用慢火爆香，滑下鷄件兜炒片刻加薯仔，水及調味料同煮20分鐘，慢慢流入椰汁煮沸即成。

Ingredients:

1 serai (lemon grass) – 4" needed
2 large onions
5 tbsp oil
2 to 3 tbsp curry powder
1 tsp turmeric powder
2 slices ginger
3 garlic cloves
2 tsp balachan (shrimp paste)
4 chillies
1 chicken, about 3 lb (1½ kg)
2 tbsp ginger juice
2 tbsp wine
1 lb (½ kg) cooked, peeled
  potatoes
1 cup water
2 cups coconut milk

Seasoning-
1 tsp salt
1 tbsp sugar
½ tsp chicken powder

Method:

* Wash, cut and retain 4" (10 cm) of the serai. Mash and leave aside.
* Chop and put the onions into the mortar and pound into a paste.
* Add 2 tbsp of the oil into half of the curry and turmeric powder to stir into a very thick paste. Sauté the mashed onion with another tbsp of the oil till aromatic then add the curry paste to fry thoroughly.
* Using a mortar, pound the serai, ginger, garlic, balachan and chillies into a smooth paste. Mix well with the curry and onion purée.

* Cut the chicken into large
  chunks then marinate in the
  ginger juice, wine, and the
  remaining curry powder for 1
  hour.
* Heat the wok with the remaining
  oil. Pour in the mixture to stir fry

over low heat until pungent.
Slide in the chicken to stir fry for
a while. Add the potatoes, water
and seasoning to simmer for 20
minutes. Stream in the coconut
milk to bring to boil again. Dish
and serve.

白　切　鷄
Poached Chicken

材料：

水20杯
上鷄1只約3磅（1½公斤）
麻油塗面

調味—羌汁2湯匙
　　　酒2湯匙
　　　鹽2湯匙
　　　糖1湯匙

醮料—羌1安（28克）
　　　葱茸½安（14克）
　　　鹽2湯匙
　　　糖1茶匙
　　　沸油2湯匙

製法：

* 深鍋內放清水煮沸。加入羌汁、酒
　、鹽及糖，試妥味後隨將洗淨之鷄
　放入，待水煮沸時，停火蓋上鍋蓋
　浸30分鐘。

* 將鷄取出，置水喉下不斷沖水約30
　分鐘，滴乾水份，以毛巾抹乾。塗
　以麻油後斬件上碟，排成鷄之原狀
　。

* 羌洗淨磨成茸，放在小碟中，加葱
　茸、幼鹽、糖撈勻，潶下沸油，即
　可與鷄同上。

Ingredients:

20 cups water
1 chicken, about 3 lb (1½ kg)
sesame oil for brushing

Seasoning-
2 tbsp ginger juice
2 tbsp wine
2 tbsp salt
1 tbsp sugar

Dipping-
1 oz (28 g) ginger
1/2 oz (14 g) chopped chives
2 tbsp salt
1 tsp sugar
2 tbsp hot oil

Method:

* Bring the water to boil in a deep saucepan. Season with the ginger juice, wine, salt and sugar. Clean the chicken and put in the cleaned seasoned water. Reboil and turn off the heat. Leave the chicken to soak in the hot soup with the lid on for 30 minutes.

* Remove the chicken and place under a running tap to refresh for 30 to 60 minutes. Drain and dry with a towel. Brush the sesame oil over the whole carcass then chop into serving pieces. Arrange into the original shape of a chicken on a platter.

* Clean and grate the ginger to put in a small dish. Add the chopped chives, salt, sugar and the hot oil to mix well and serve as a dipping.

芝 蔴 鷄

Sesame Chicken

材料：

鷄肉8安（224克）
肥肉10安（280克）
沸水2杯
生粉2湯匙
芝蔴3安（84克）
芫茜葉作裝飾
炸油4杯

醃料—羌汁1茶匙
　　　酒1茶匙
　　　生粉1茶匙
　　　胡椒粉少許
　　　蛋白½隻

調味—鹽⅓茶匙
　　　糖½茶匙
　　　蔴油1茶匙

製法：

＊　鷄肉洗淨抹乾剁成肉茸，加醃料和
　　勻醃10分鐘，拌入調味料搓勻。
＊　肥肉置沸水中焓10分鐘，冲凍後切
　　成1½×2吋（3.75×5公分）薄片
　　。
＊　生粉塗勻在肥肉上，再將鷄茸鋪在
　　上面。鷄茸上洒滿芝蔴 以手按緊，
　　芫茜葉1片釀在上面裝飾。
＊　燒紅鑊，倒下炸油燒熱。滑下鷄件
　　，以文火炸至金黃色，排在碟中。
　　花椒粉及喼汁跟上。

Ingredients:

8 oz (224 g) chicken meat
10 oz (280 g) fat pork
2 cups boiling water
2 tbsp cornflour
3 oz (84 g) sesame seeds
parley to garnish
4 cups oil for deep frying

Marinade-　　　Seasoning-
1 tsp ginger juice　1/3 tsp salt
1 tsp wine　　　1/2 tsp sugar
1 tsp cornflour　1 tsp sesame oil
1/8 tsp pepper
1/2 egg white

Method:

* *Wash and mince the chicken meat into a purée. Immerse in the marinade and leave to stand for 10 minutes. Blend in the seasoning and pound until springy.*
* *Cook the fat pork in the boiling water for 10 minutes. Refresh and slice into 1¹/₂" x 2" (3.75 cm x 5 cm) thin pieces.*
* *Dust each piece of fat pork with a little cornflour then pile the chicken purée on top. Sprinkle the sesame seeds over the chicken then garnish with a parsley leaf. Press lightly to secure.*
* *Gently bring the oil to just boil. Deep fry the chicken till light brown. Remove and drain. Arrange on a platter to serve with xanthoxylum seed powder and Worchestershire sauce.*

蠔 油 焗 鷄

Stewed Chicken in Oyster Sauce

材料：

鷄腿20安（560克）
老抽2湯匙
熟冬菇10隻
紅蘿葡4安（112克）
羌片數塊
葱頭2粒
蒜頭2粒
芫茜3棵
炸油3杯

調味—酒2茶匙
　　　上湯1杯
　　　生抽1茶匙
　　　蠔油2湯匙
　　　糖1茶匙
　　　胡椒粉少許

饋料—生粉1茶匙
　　　水1湯匙
　　　老抽½茶匙

製法：

* 鷄腿洗淨抹乾，用老抽塗在鷄上。
* 冬菇斜刀片開，紅蘿葡飛水切片，羌、葱、蒜頭剁茸；芫茜摘妥。
* 燒紅鑊倒下炸油煮沸，將鷄放入炸至淺黃時撈起，倒去餘油。
* 鑊中餘油少許燒熱投入羌片、葱頭、蒜頭、紅蘿葡、冬菇，潰下酒，即加上湯及調味品，同時將鷄放入，蓋上鑊蓋，焗五分鐘。取出斬件，餘汁加饋料煮濃，淋在鷄件上，以芫茜裝飾。

Ingredients:

20 oz (560 g) chicken thighs
2 tbsp dark soy
10 cooked Chinese mushrooms
4 oz (112 g) carrot
3 slices ginger
2 shallots
2 garlic cloves
3 parsley sprigs
3 cups oil for deep frying

Seasoning-	Gravy Mix-
2 tsp sherry	1 tsp cornflour
1 cup stock	1 tbsp water
1 tsp light soy	½ tsp dark soy
2 tbsp oyster sauce	
1 tsp sugar	
⅛ tsp pepper	

Method:

* Clean and dry the chicken with a towel. Brush evenly with the dark soy.
* Slice the mushrooms. Blanch and slice the carrot. Mince the ginger, shallots and garlic. Trim the parsley.
* Bring the oil to boil in a heated wok to deep fry the chicken until golden brown. Drain and leave 2 tbsp of oil in the wok.
* Reheat the oil in the wok to sauté the ginger, shallots and garlic. Sizzle the sherry then pour in the stock and seasoning. Return the chicken into the wok. Add the mushrooms and carrot to simmer for 5 minutes. Remove the chicken on to a chopping board and cut into

pieces. Arrange on a platter with
the mushrooms and carrot.
Thicken the sauce with the gravy
mix. Pour over the chicken and
serve hot. Garnish with the
parsley.

鮮　竹　卷
Crisp Bean Curd Rolls

材料：

蝦仁6安（168克）
溫油3杯
豬肉6安（168克）
熟冬菇2安（56克）
紅蘿蔔4安（112克）
葱頭1粒切片
腐皮2張

醃料—生抽2茶匙
　　　生粉1茶匙
　　　糖1茶匙
　　　酒½茶匙
　　　水2湯匙

調味—酒1茶匙
　　　水3湯匙
　　　生抽1½茶匙
　　　糖1茶匙
　　　蔴油1茶匙
　　　胡椒粉少許
　　　生粉水1茶匙

製法：

* 蝦去腸臟洗淨，以毛巾吸乾水份，放入溫油中泡片刻，隔去餘油留用。
* 豬肉切絲以醃料撈勻後泡油待用，將油留下炸腐皮。
* 冬菇切絲。紅蘿蔔飛水後切絲。
* 燒紅鑊加油2湯匙爆香葱頭片，倒下全部材料。讚酒傾入水及調味料，試妥味後，以生粉埋饘盛起攤凍。
* 每張腐皮剪為6個三角形。將以上油煮沸放入腐皮炸至金黃色，取出浸在一盆凍水中至軟。以毛巾抹乾，包入餡料2湯匙，摺成長卷形。置油鑊中煎至金黃色上碟。

Ingredients:

6 oz (168 g) shelled shrimps
3 cups warm oil
6 oz (168 g) pork
2 oz (56 g) fresh mushrooms
4 oz (112 g) carrot
1 sliced shallot
2 bean curd sheets

Mariande-	Seasoning-
2 tsp light soy	1 tsp wine
1 tsp cornflour	3 tbsp water
1 tsp sugar	1 1/2 tsp light soy
1/2 tsp wine	1 tsp sugar
2 tbsp water	1 tsp sesame oil
	1/8 tsp pepper
	1 tsp cornflour mix

Method:

* Devein and wash the shrimps. Dry thoroughly with a towel then parboil in the warm oil and drain. Leave aside and keep the oil for later use.
* Shred the pork then immerse in the marinade for 20 minutes. Parboil in the above warm oil and leave aside. Keep the oil for later use.
* Blanch and shred the mushrooms and carrot.
* Heat the wok with 2 tbsp of the oil to sauté the shallot till fragrant. Stir in all the ingredients. Sizzle the wine; add the water and seasoning. Adjust the flavor to taste. Thicken the sauce with the cornflour mix.
* Cut each bean curd sheet into 6 triangles. Bring the oil to boil and deep fry the bean curd sheets till crisp. Remove into a bowl of water to soak until soft then dry with a clean towel. Place 2 tbsp filling on one side and fold into a roll. Shallow fry in a heated wok with 1 tbsp oil. Serve hot.

鬆 化 蛋 散
Crisp Waffle

材料：

根粉½磅（¼公斤）
發粉1茶匙
梳打粉½茶匙
鷄蛋3只
生粉作培
油½鍋
糖膠適量

製法：

* 　根粉、發粉、梳打粉一同篩在桌上，撥開一穴。
* 　鷄蛋打爛後倒在穴內，輕輕用手將四週之麵粉撥入，搓勻成一軟麵團。
* 　將麵團以木棍開成長方形，拍上生粉，兩塊叠在一起輾薄。用刀切成1½″×4″長條形，中央剪三條縫，穿過反轉。
* 　燒紅鑊放入油大半鍋煮沸，將蛋散放入，炸至微黃即以罩籬捞起，倒下糖膠。

Ingredients:

8 oz (224 g) high protein flour
1 tsp baking powder
¹/₂ tsp soda bicarbonate
3 large eggs
cornflour for dusting
¹/₂ wok oil for deep frying
corn syrup for coating

Method:

* *Sift the flour, baking powder and soda bicarbonate on the pastry board and make a well in the centre.*
* *Beat the eggs and drop into the well. Slowly draw in the flour to knead into a soft and smooth dough.*
* *Roll the dough into a rectangle then dust with the cornflour. Fold and roll until a very thin sheet is formed. Cut into strips of 1¹/₂" x 4" (3.75 cm x 10 cm). Make 3 slits in the middle of each piece and pull one end through the centre slit.*
* *Fill a hot wok with the oil and bring to the boil. Slide in the strips to deep fry until golden brown. Remove and drain on absorbent paper. Pour the syrup over each waffle and serve at once.*

銀 針 粉
Silver Pin Noodles with Shrimps

材料：

油 4 湯匙
銀針粉 10 安（280克）
蝦仁 4 安（112克）
豬肉絲 4 安（112克）
溫油 2 杯
白菌 4 粒
沸水 1 杯
青豆 ½ 杯
芽菜 6 安（168克）
蛋皮一張切絲

醃料一生抽 1 茶匙
　　　生粉 1 茶匙
　　　酒 ½ 茶匙
　　　糖 ½ 茶匙
　　　水 2 湯匙

調味一酒 1 茶匙
　　　鹽 ¼ 茶匙
　　　生抽 2 茶匙
　　　糖 1 茶匙
　　　胡椒粉少許
　　　蔴油 ½ 茶匙

製法：

* 燒紅鑊加油 2 湯匙，將銀針粉爆香盛起候用。
* 蝦去腸洗淨抹乾。
* 肉絲以醃料醃20分鐘，置溫油內泡 ½ 分鐘後，隔去餘油。
* 白菌切絲，置沸水中與青豆同飛水沖凍隔乾。
* 燒紅鑊加入餘油，爆香芽菜倒入全部材料炒勻。將銀針粉放回鑊中，**濳酒**加調味料試妥味，隨即下蛋皮絲兜勻上碟。

Ingredients:

4 tbsp oil
10 oz (280 g) silver pin noodles
4 oz (112 g) shelled shrimps
4 oz (112 g) shredded pork
2 cups warm oil
4 fresh mushrooms
1 cup boiling water
¼ cup sweet peas
6 oz (168 g) bean sprouts
1 shredded egg sheet

Marinade-
1 tsp light soy
1 tsp cornflour
½ tsp wine
½ tsp sugar
2 tbsp water

Seasoning-
1 tsp wine
¼ tsp salt
2 tsp light soy
1 tsp sugar
⅛ tsp pepper
½ tsp sesame oil

Method:

* Heat 2 tbsp of the oil in a hot wok to shallow fry the noodles. Dish and leave aside.
* Devein, clean and dry the shrimps.
* Immerse the pork in the marinade for 20 minutes. Parboil in the warm oil and drain.
* Shred the mushrooms and blanch in the boiling water with the sweet peas. Refresh and drain.
* Heat the wok with the remaining

oil. Sauté the bean sprouts for a
short while then add all the other
ingredients to fry evenly. Return
the noodles into the wok. Sizzle
the wine and season to taste. Stir
in the shredded egg sheet to mix
well. Remove and dish.

鮮 蝦 粉 菓
Steamed Raviolis

材料：

皮－汀麵4安（112克）　調味－酒1茶匙
　　沸水½杯　　　　　　　鹽¼茶匙
　　鹽¼茶匙　　　　　　　生抽1茶匙
　　油½茶匙　　　　　　　糖1茶匙
　　　　　　　　　　　　　蔴油少許
餡料－蝦4安（112克）
　　生粉2茶匙
　　胡椒粉少許
　　瘦肉4安（112克）
　　紅蘿蔔2安（56克）
　　熟冬菇2隻
　　芫茜茸1茶匙
　　油1湯匙

製法：

皮－
＊　澄麵篩在盆中，將沸水冲入加鹽快
　　手搞勻。用蓋蓋着1分鐘。取出置
　　枱上，加油搓成一軟糰，以毛巾蓋
　　住候用。

餡－
＊　蝦洗淨切粒，用一半生粉及胡椒粉
　　撈勻。
＊　瘦肉切粒，以餘下生粉醃片刻。
＊　紅蘿蔔飛水後與冬菇一同切指甲片
　　。
＊　燒紅鑊加油，爆香瘦肉及蝦。傾入
　　其他材料及芫茜，潷酒洒調味料和
　　勻盛起。

完成－
＊　澄麵搓成長條切成32粒。以木棍開
　　成圓形包入餡料1湯匙收緊。置已
　　塗油之蒸籠內中火蒸4分鐘，熱食
　　。

Ingredients:

Pastry-
4 oz (112 g) wheat starch
1/2 cup boiling water
1/4 tsp salt
1/2 tsp oil

Filling-　　　　*Seasoning-*
4 oz (112 g) shrimps　*1 tsp sherry*
2 tsp cornflour　　*1/4 tsp salt*
1/8 tsp pepper　　*1 tsp light soy*
4 oz (112 g) lean pork　*1 tsp sugar*
2 oz (56 g) carrot　*1/2 tsp sesame oil*
2 cooked mushrooms
1 tsp chopped parsley
1 tbsp oil

Method:

Pastry-
* Sift the wheat starch into a mixing bowl and stir in the boiling water and the salt till evenly mixed. Cover the bowl with a lid for 1 minute. Remove on to the table to knead into a soft dough. Add the oil to knead well. Cover with a towel and leave aside.

Filling-
* Clean, dice and coat the shrimps with half the cornflour and pepper.
* Dice and marinate the pork with the remaining cornflour.
* Blanch and dice the carrot. Dice the mushrooms.
* Heat a wok with the oil to sauté the pork and shrimps for a while. Stir in the other ingredients and parsley. Sizzle the wine and season to taste.

To Complete-
* Knead the dough to form a long cylinder. Cut into 32 small equal portions and press each into a round. Place 1 tsp filling in each round and wrap up securely. Cook in a greased steamer for 4 minutes. Serve hot.

芋　頭　糕
Taro Pudding

材料：

芋頭2磅（1公斤）
生油¼杯
水4至6杯
蝦米2安（56克）
冬菇數隻
臘肉½磅（224克）
臘腸2條（隨意）
粘粉½磅（224克）
葱粒1湯匙

調味—胡椒粉¼茶匙
　　　五香粉1茶匙
　　　鹽1½湯匙
　　　糖2湯匙

製法：

* 芋頭去皮洗淨刨絲，以豬油起鑊煮軟，水逐漸加入至濃度適中。
* 冬菇蝦米浸軟切幼，臘肉切粒分別爆香後加入芋絲中煮，古月粉五香粉及調味品加入撈勻。
* 粘米粉用篩篩入同搞。
* 糕盆塗油倒入糕料放置大火蒸籠內蒸約1小時。取出用塗油湯匙將糕面燙平，洒下葱粒攤凍。食時切片放入油鑊中煎至金黃色。與蠔油同上。

Ingredients:

2 lb (1 kg) taro
¼ cup oil
4 – 6 cups water
2 oz (56 g) dried shrimps
4 Chinese mushrooms
½ lb (224 g) bacon
2 Chinese sausages (optional)
8 oz (224 g) rice flour
1 tbsp chopped chives

Seasoning-
¼ tsp pepper
1 tsp five spice powder
1½ tbsp salt
2 tbsp sugar

Method:

* *Peel and shred the taro. Heat the wok with the oil to sauté the taro till soft. Add the water to simmer for 15 minutes.*
* *Wash and soak the mushrooms and shrimps till soft. Dice the mushrooms, shrimps, bacon and sausages. Stir fry in a hot wok then mix with the cooked taro.*
* *Sift in the flour to bind into a thick batter. Season to taste. Pour into a greased cake mould and place in a steamer to cook over high heat for an hour. Remove and smoothen the top with a greased spoon then sprinkle the chopped chives on it. Leave to cool.*
* *Shallow fry the sliced taro pudding in an oiled pan till golden brown. Serve hot with oyster sauce.*

馬　蹄　糕
Water Chestnut Pudding

材料：

生馬蹄1磅（½公斤）
糖12安（336克）
水6杯
馬蹄粉10安（280克）
油2湯匙

製法：

* 馬蹄去皮洗淨磨碎，放鍋中加糖及水4
* 清水2杯開馬蹄粉，用茶隔隔去雜質，加入豬油搞勻。
* 將馬蹄粉液慢慢倒入馬蹄糖水中，邊倒邊搞。
* 搞勻後倒入塗油之糕盆內，然後放入蒸籠內大火蒸約40分鐘，取出攤凍。

Ingredients:

1 lb (¹/₂ kg) water chestnuts
12 oz (336 g) sugar
6 cups water
10 oz (280 g) water chestnut starch
2 tbsp oil

Method:

* *Peel and wash the water chestnuts. Grate and cook in 4 cups of the water with the sugar for 10 minutes.*
* *Mix the water chestnut starch with the remaining 2 cups of water then filter through a fine sieve.*
* *Pour the starch mix with the oil gradually into the boiling syrup. Stir constantly until well mixed. Scoop into a greased cake mould and steam over medium heat for 40 minutes. Leave to cool.*
* *Cut into oblong pieces to shallow fry in an oiled pan before serving.*

黑椒牛柳
Black Pepper Steak

材料：

牛柳2件各重6安（168克）
牛油3湯匙
乾葱2粒
蒜頭2粒
洋葱1只
茨菜1杯

調味一白蘭地2湯匙
　　　鹽½茶匙
　　　糖1茶匙
　　　黃汁1杯
　　　黑椒粉隨意

Ingredients:

2 fillet steaks, each 6 oz (168 g)
3 tbsp butter
2 shallots
2 garlic cloves
1 onion
1 cup mixed vegetables

Seasoning-
2 tbsp brandy
1/2 tsp salt
1 tsp sugar
1 cup brown sauce
black pepper to taste

製法：

* 牛柳起去四週筋絡，修好抹乾。
* 將牛柳切成每件約1½″厚，以毛巾包住拍鬆。
* 平底鑊燒熱放入牛油煮沸，把牛柳放入猛火煎至兩面金黃色及硬身。
* 乾葱、洋葱、蒜頭皆去衣，剁爛成茸，放在燒紅之油鑊內爆香，加黑椒粉拌勻，潑下白蘭地酒，鑊中着火時即將牛柳放入，兩邊稍煎，即可盛在燒熱之碟上，碟旁放置茨菜。
* 黃汁加入鑊中與餘汁和勻煮沸，以盅盛起同上，或直接淋在牛柳上。

Method:

* *Trim and absorb the excess moisture on the steaks with a kitchen towel.*
* *Wrap the meat in the towel and shape into 1½" (3.75 cm) thick round pieces.*
* *Heat the pan with the butter then sear both sides of the steaks over high heat.*
* *Mince the shallots, garlic and onion and sauté in the buttered pan. Drop in the brandy and season to taste. Return the steaks into the flaming pan immediately to fry for 2 seconds. Remove on to a hot iron plate. Arrange the mixed vegetables on one side.*
* *Blend the brown sauce into the remaining liquid in the frying pan. Simmer for 1 minute then adjust the seasoning according to taste. Pour over the steaks or serve separately in a gravy boat.*

龍　蝦　沙　律
Lobster Salad

材料：

龍蝦1隻重2磅（1公斤）
薯仔10安（280克）
紅蘿蔔10安（280克）
鷄蛋2只
靑瓜1條
萍果2只
番茄1只
靑豆4安（112克）

沙律醬料—蛋黃16隻
　　　　　鹽2茶匙
　　　　　糖3茶匙
　　　　　芥末粉3茶匙
　　　　　胡椒粉½茶匙
　　　　　油1杯
　　　　　醋¾杯
　　　　　花奶數滴

製法：

* 龍蝦放入已燒沸之水中煮20分鐘，取出去殼切片。
* 薯仔、紅蘿蔔、鷄蛋洗淨烚熟，去皮切粒。
* 靑瓜去籽切粒，萍果去皮去心切粒。
* 番茄洗淨切粒，靑豆出水後留用。

沙律醬—

* 蛋黃加鹽、糖、芥末粉、古月粉等打至奶油狀，將粟米油逐滴加入同攪，邊攪邊加，攪至濃時方逐加醋同攪，最後加花奶調勻。
* 將各種蔬菓粒一同混合加沙律醬撈勻，龍蝦頭放在碟上，混好之蔬菓粒放置碟中，上舖龍蝦片，用幼唧咀將沙律醬唧在龍蝦片上。

（如不欲自製沙律醬，可在超級市場購1瓶）

Ingredients:

1/2 wok water
1 lobster, about 2 lb (1 kg)
10 oz (280 g) potatoes
10 oz (280 g) carrots
2 eggs
1 cucumber
2 apples
1 tomato
4 oz (112 g) sweet peas

Mayonnaise-
16 egg yolks
2 tsp salt
3 tsp sugar
3 tsp mustard powder
1/2 tsp white pepper
1 cup oil
3/4 cup vinegar
a few drops evaporated milk

Method:

* *Bring the water to boil over high heat. Put in the lobster to cook for 20 minutes. Remove the shell and slice.*
* *Wash, cook and peel the potatoes, carrots and eggs. Dice.*
* *Peel and dice the cucumber and apples.*
* *Peel and dice the tomato. Blanch and refresh the sweet peas.*

Mayonnaise-
* *Place the egg yolks in a mixing bowl to whisk with the salt, sugar, mustard and white pep-*

per till creamy. Drop in the oil
gradually and stir until thic-
kened. Adjust to a dropping
consistency with the vinegar.
Finally stir in the evaporated
milk.
* Mix all the diced ingredients
with the mayonnaise then place
on a paltter. Arrange the lobster
head at one end of the platter
and the tail at the other. Top the
diced ingredients with the sliced
lobster. Garnish with more
mayonnaise.

肉 丸 意 粉
Spaghetti with Meatballs

材料：

意粉½磅（224克）
油4湯匙
茄汁⅛杯
牛肉½磅（224克）
洋葱1只
麵包2片
蛋1隻
麵粉1湯匙
沸油4杯
蒜茸1湯匙
洋葱粒¼杯
西芹粒½杯
黃汁¼杯
茄糕¼杯
香葉1片

調味—酒1茶匙
　　　水1杯
　　　鹽1茶匙
　　　糖2茶匙
　　　胡椒粉少許

製法：

* 意粉放沸水內，加鹽1湯匙焓15分鐘，倒出隔去水份，過冷河隔乾。
* 燒紅鑊，放入油2湯匙煮沸，將意粉倒下，加茄汁少許兜勻，盛在碟上。
* 牛肉用刀攪攪成肉茸，洋葱剁成茸，麵包浸軟，加調味品一同攪透。再加蛋1隻及麵粉和勻做成肉丸，置沸油內炸至金黃色。
* 燒紅鑊加入餘油2湯匙煮沸，爆香蒜茸，倒入洋葱粒及西芹粒兜炒片刻。灒酒加水，黃汁、茄糕及香葉一同煮沸。將肉丸重放入同煮10分鐘，盛起淋在意粉上即成。

Ingredients:

1/2 lb (224 g) spaghetti
4 cups boiling salted water
4 tbsp butter
1/8 cup tomato ketchup
1/2 lb (224 g) beef
1 onion
2 slices bread
1 egg
1 tbsp flour
4 cups hot oil
1 tbsp minced garlic
1/4 cup chopped onion
1/2 cup chopped celery
1/4 cup brown sauce
1/4 cup tomato purée
1 bay leaf

Seasoning-
1 tsp wine
1 cup water
1 tsp salt
2 tsp sugar
1/8 tsp pepper

Method:

* *Cook the spaghetti in the boiling salted water for 15 minutes. Drain.*
* *Bring 2 tbsp of the butter to boil in the wok. Pour in the spaghetti and tomato ketchup to mix well. Remove and dish.*
* *Wash and mince the beef. Chop the onion finely. Soak the bread in a little water. Place all these in a mixing bowl to mix well with some seasoning. Blend in the egg and flour and shape into meatballs. Deep fry in the hot oil till golden brown.*

* *Heat the wok to bring the remaining butter to boil. Sauté the garlic till aromatic. Add the onion and celery to stir fry for a while. Sizzle the wine; add the water, brown sauce, tomato* *purée and the bay leaf to bring to boil. Return the meatballs into the sauce to simmer for 10 minutes. Spoon over the spaghetti and serve.*

聖 誕 釀 鵝
Stuffed Christmas Goose

材料：

鵝1隻（約5磅）（2½公斤）

鵝 餡—栗子1磅（½公斤）調味—鹽3茶匙
　　洋蔥6安（168克）　　　　糖2茶匙
　　西芹6安（168克）　　　　雞粉1茶匙
　　油3湯匙
　　牛肉8安（224克）塗料—羌汁2湯匙
　　豬肉8安（224克）　　　白酒2湯匙
　　煙肉6安（168克）　　　喼汁2湯匙
　　麵粉½杯十水

汁 料—水4杯
　　鵝雜掌翼及部份骨
　　西芹2安（56克）
　　紅蘿蔔片2安（56克）
　　黃汁½杯
　　鹽½茶匙

製法：

* 將鵝由背中間劏開，取出內臟退去
　骨頭，只留四柱骨（四肢）。鵝雜
　、掌翼及骨留作煮汁用。栗子去殼
　煮熟挾爛成茸。
* 將洋蔥、西芹切成茸。
* 燒紅鑊，加油、洋蔥、西芹、栗子
　略炒後盛起。
* 牛肉、豬肉、煙肉同搞爛。加調味
　料醃片刻。倒入熱鑊中略炒，繼將
　洋蔥、西芹、栗子茸拌入和勻，再
　將麵粉加水開成濃漿傾下撈勻調妥
　味。
* 將已炒好之鵝餡置放在鵝皮內，釀
　八分滿，用幼白繩將鵝背縫好。
* 在鵝皮外以白酒、喼汁塗勻，吹乾
　。放在已塗油燒熱之焗盤內以300
　度火焗至金黃，約半小時反身一次
　塗油，大約2小時即可取出，切片
　上碟。以番茄、青瓜片、芫茜伴碟
　邊。

汁料—

* 深鍋1個加水將汁料放入（黃汁及
　鹽除外），以慢火熬1小時，隔去
　渣滓。加黃汁及鹽拌勻跟上。

Ingredients:

1 goose, about 5 lb (2¹/₂ kg)

Stuffing-
1 lb (¹/₂ kg) chestnuts
6 oz (168 g) chopped onions
6 oz (168 g) chopped celery
3 tbsp oil
8 oz (224 g) minced beef
8 oz (224 g) minced pork
6 oz (168 g) minced bacon
¹/₂ cup flour mixed with water

Seasoning-
3 tsp salt
2 tsp sugar
1 tsp chicken powder

Coating Sauce-
2 tbsp ginger juice
2 tbsp white wine
2 tbsp Worchestershire Sauce

Gravy-
4 cups water
1 gizzard
¹/₂ lb (224g) goose bones
the wings and legs of the goose
2 oz (56 g) sliced celery
2 oz (56 g) sliced carrot
¹/₂ cup brown sauce
¹/₂ tsp salt

Method:

* Clean and debone the goose. Retain the gizzard, wings, legs and the bones for the gravy. Shell, cook and mash the chestnuts.
* Heat 2 tbsp of the oil in a hot wok to sauté the onion, celery and chestnuts.
* Marinate the beef and pork with half of the seasoning for 20 minutes. Shallow fry in the remaining oil then add the onions, celery, chestnuts and bacon to mix evenly. Stream in the flour mix and seasoning to stir thoroughly.
* Stuff the goose with the above ingredients until it is ¾ full. Sew up the opening.

* Brush the goose skin with the coating sauce then hang up to dry. Put the goose on to a greased hot baking tray and bake in a 300°F (Gas Mark 2) oven until golden. Turn every 30 minutes and baste with the dripping. Cook for 2 hours. Slice and arrange on a dish. Garnish with sliced tomatoes, cucumber and parsley if desired.

Gravy—
* Bring the water to boil in a saucepan with all the sauce ingredients except the brown sauce and the salt. Simmer for 1 hour over low heat. Filter the sauce through a sieve, add the brown sauce and salt. Mix well and serve separately.

焗 釀 乳 鴿
Stuffed Pigeons

材料：

洋葱 1 個	飯 1 杯
西芹 1 片	乳鴿 3 隻
鷄肝 2 副	生抽 2 湯匙
羌汁 1 茶匙	雜菜½杯
生粉 1 茶匙	炸茨條½杯

調味— 酒 1 茶匙
　　　 鹽¼茶匙
　　　 生抽 2 茶匙
　　　 糖 1 茶匙
　　　 胡椒粉少許
　　　 鷄粉½茶匙

製法：

* 洋葱、西芹剁爛成茸，鷄肝亦剁爛
  成茸，以羌汁及生粉略醃。
* 燒紅鑊，爆香洋葱及西芹茸，盛起。
* 再燒紅鑊爆鷄肝茸，加入調味品和
  勻，然後加入已爆好之洋葱西芹茸
  及白飯，炒香盛起。
* 乳鴿擦淨皮，用小刀退骨後洗淨。
  將飯釀入鴿皮內，以針縫開口處，
  外皮塗以生抽。
* 焗盤燒熱塗油，放入乳鴿用 300 度
  火焗至金黃色，配什菜上碟。

Ingredients:

1 onion
1 celery stick
2 chicken livers
1 tsp ginger juice
1 tsp cornflour
2 tbsp oil
1 cup cooked rice
3 pigeons
2 tbsp light soy
1/2 cup mixed vegetables
1 cup fried potato chips

Seasoning-
1 tsp wine
1/4 tsp salt
2 tsp light soy
1 tsp sugar
1/8 tsp pepper
1/2 tsp chicken powder

Method:

* Finely chop the onion and celery. Dice the chicken livers
  finely, then marinate with the
  ginger juice and cornflour.
* Heat a wok with 1 tbsp of the oil
  to sauté the onion and celery till
  aromatic. Leave aside for later
  use.
* Reheat the wok with the remaining oil to shallow fry the chicken
  livers. Sizzle the wine and add
  the seasoning to mix well.
  Return the onion and celery into
  the wok. Add the cooked rice to
  stir fry until thoroughly mixed
  then remove.
* Debone the pigeons. Wash and
  towel dry. Stuff the birds with
  the fried rice then sew up the
  opening. Brush the skin with the
  light soy.
* Grease a baking tray to put in
  the pigeons then bake in a preheated 300°F (Gas Mark 2) oven
  till golden.
* Blanch the mixed vegetables and
  serve the stuffed pigeons with the
  fried potato chips.

椰撻
Coconut Tarts

材料：

皮—麵粉8安（224克）
　　硬牛油5安（140克）
　　冰水2湯匙

餡—糖6安（168克）
　　沸水½杯
　　牛油1½安（42克）
　　椰茸4安（112克）
　　蛋液2隻
　　淡奶1湯匙
　　香油數滴
　　發粉½茶匙
　　車厘子片數粒

製法：

皮—
* 麵粉篩在桌上，放入硬牛油在粉中搓碎，以指尖擦成麵包糠一樣，加入冰水搓匀候用。

餡—
* 糖加水煮溶後續滾5分鐘，停火放入牛油自溶。
* 牛油溶後加入椰茸搞匀，攤凍後打入雞蛋搞匀，再加花奶，香油及發粉拌匀。
* 將椰茸餡攤凍，放雪櫃內雪1小時。

完成—
* 粉糰用木棍輾薄，用花級級出，放撻盞內用手捏好，中放椰茸餡約七分滿，以車厘子點綴。
* 焗爐開定300度，將椰撻放入焗約40分鐘。

Ingredients:

Pastry-
8 oz (224 g) flour
5 oz (140 g) butter
2 tbsp iced water

Filling-
6 oz (168 g) sugar
1/2 cup boiling water
1 1/2 oz (42 g) butter
4 oz (112 g) desiccated coconut
2 beaten eggs
1 tbsp milk
1/8 tsp vanilla essence
1/2 tsp baking powder
sliced cherries for decoration

Method:

Pastry-
* *Sift the flour on to the table and rub in the butter to form fine bread crumbs. Mix well with the iced water then knead into a soft dough. Leave aside for later use.*

Filling-
* *Dissolve the sugar in the boiling water. Continue to simmer for 5 minutes. Drop in the butter and leave to melt.*
* *Stir in the desiccated coconut after the butter has melted. Leave to cool for a while then add the beaten eggs to mix with the milk, vanilla essence and baking powder.*
* *Chilli in the refrigerator for an hour.*

To complete —
* Lay the dough on to a lightly
  floured board to roll out into a
  thin piece. Cut into rounds with
  a cutter. Line each tart case with
  the pastry and put in the filling,
  about 3/4 full. Decorate with the
  sliced cherries.

* Arrange the tart cases on a baking sheet and put in the middle
  shelf of a preheated 300°F oven
  (Gas Mark 2) to bake for 40
  minutes.

炸 鷄 角
Deep Fried Chicken Triangles

材料：

皮—麵粉8安（224克）
　　鹽¼茶匙
　　胡椒粉少許
　　硬牛油1½安（42克）
　　硬豬油2安（56克）
　　凍水1安（28克）
　　蛋1隻打爛
　　炸油½鑊

餡—油1湯匙
　　洋葱粒1個
　　熟鷄肉粒4安（112克）
　　白汁½杯

製法：

皮—
* 麵粉、鹽及胡椒粉一同篩在桌上。
* 放入牛油、豬油擦碎成粉末，加入
　凍水和勻，搓成軟糰。

餡—
* 燒紅鑊加油煮沸爆香洋葱粒。停火
　加入切碎之熟鷄肉撈勻，再加白汁
　拌成餡料。取出放置一旁。

完成—
* 麵糰用木棍開薄，級成5吋（12.5
　公分）圓形，將一湯匙餡料放在一
　邊覆轉以蛋液塗邊，將餡包住，捏
　成角形。
* 將油煮至僅沸。轉用中火，將鷄角
　放入炸至金黃色，撈起隔去餘油。

Ingredients:

Pastry-
8 oz (224 g) flour
¼ tsp salt
⅛ tsp pepper
1½ oz (42 g) chilled butter
2 oz (56 g) chilled lard
⅛ cup cold water
1 beaten egg
½ wok oil for deep frying

Filling-
1 tbsp oil
1 diced onion
*4 oz (112 g) diced cooked chicken
　meat*
½ cup white sauce

Method:

Pastry-
* *Sift the flour, salt and pepper on
　to the table.*
* *Rub in the butter and lard with
　your finger tips then add the cold
　water to knead into a smooth
　dough.*

Filling-
* *Heat the wok with the oil to
　sauté the onion. Turn off the
　heat and stir in the chicken. Add
　the white sauce to bind all the
　ingredients together. Remove
　and leave aside.*

To Complete-
* *Roll the dough into a thin piece and cut into 5" (12.5 cm) rounds. Put 1 tbsp of the filling on one side of each piece of dough then fold and seal with the beaten egg.*

* *Bring the oil to just boil. Deep fry the chicken triangles till golden brown. Remove and drain on absorbent paper.*

炸　蛋　球
Deep Fried Egg Balls

材料：

水10安（280克）
豬油1安（28克）
麵粉6安（168克）
臭粉¾茶匙
鷄蛋5只
幼糖1杯洒面

製法：

* 將水與豬油同放鍋內煮沸。
* 停火立刻倒入麵粉，迅速以木棍搞拌。
* 加入臭粉及鷄蛋，加一只蛋搞拌一次，至完全混合妥當。
* 油一鍋放在爐上，慢火煮至開始暖時即可逐匙將蛋漿放入，慢慢炸至三倍大。
* 幼糖放在碗中，將蛋球立刻投入滾滿糖粒。

Ingredients:

10 oz (280 g) water
1 oz (28 g) lard
6 oz (168 g) flour
¾ tsp ammonia powder
5 eggs
½ wok oil for deep frying
1 cup sugar

Method:

* *Bring the water and lard to boil in a small saucepan.*
* *Turn off the heat and sift in the flour immediately, stirring at the same time.*

* *Blend in the ammonia powder to mix well. Beat in the eggs one at a time until thoroughly blended.*
* *Pour the oil in to the wok. Immediately drop in the batter 1 tbsp at a time to deep fry in the cool oil until the egg balls are three times their original size. Remove and drain on absorbent paper.*
* *Coat the egg balls evenly with the sugar and serve hot.*

炸　冬　栗
Doughnuts

材料：

牛油2湯匙
幼沙糖 $\frac{1}{2}$ 杯
雞蛋1只
鮮奶 $\frac{1}{4}$ 杯
麵粉10安（280克）
發粉1茶匙
梳打粉 $\frac{1}{2}$ 茶匙
幼鹽 $\frac{1}{4}$ 茶匙
油5杯
糖霜 $\frac{1}{2}$ 杯

製法：

* 牛油及糖放入蛋桶內打至鬆軟，將蛋加入一同打勻。
* 鮮奶加入搞勻。
* 麵粉、發粉、梳打粉及鹽篩入撈勻搓成麵糰。
* 取出麵糰用麵棍輾成 $\frac{1}{2}$ 吋（1.25公分）厚片。以冬栗級級成小圓環。
* 將油傾入鑊中燒沸，較慢火用微熱油炸至金黃色。取出隔淨餘油。以糖霜洒面。

Ingredients:

2 tbsp butter
$^{1}/_{2}$ cup sugar
1 egg
$^{1}/_{4}$ cup milk
10 oz (280 g) plain flour
1 tsp baking powder
$^{1}/_{2}$ tsp soda bicarbonate
$^{1}/_{4}$ tsp salt
5 cups oil
$^{1}/_{2}$ cup icing sugar

Method:

* *Cream the butter and sugar in a mixing bowl till fluffy and light. Beat in the egg to mix thoroughly.*
* *Add the milk to whisk well.*
* *Sift the flour, baking powder, soda and salt into the mixing bowl to bind into a soft dough.*
* *Remove the dough from the bowl and roll on a floured table top to form a pastry of about $^{1}/_{2}$" (1.25 cm) thick. Cut into rings with the doughnut cutter.*
* *Bring the oil to boil in a wok. Slide in the doughnuts to deep fry over moderate heat till golden brown. Remove and drain.*
* *Sift the icing sugar on top and serve.*

餐 包 仔
Fancy Buns

材料：

酵種—糖½茶匙
　　　溫水½杯
　　　乾發子1¼茶匙
　　　筋粉4安（112克）

麵糰—筋粉1磅（½公斤）
　　　蛋1隻
　　　糖3½安（98克）
　　　奶水2½湯匙
　　　溫水½杯
　　　溶豬油2½湯匙

塗面—蛋1隻打爛
　　　稀糖膠¼杯

製法：

酵種—
* 幼糖溶於溫水中，洒下乾發子，置溫暖地方發10分鐘至浮起。
* 筋粉篩入和勻搞成粉漿，放置一旁至粉漿發起雙倍。

麵糰—
* 筋粉篩在桌上，中間開穴放入蛋，糖及酵種一同搞勻至糖溶。慢慢將四週之粉撥入。再加奶水及溫水搓成軟糰。最後將豬油搓入，以手搓至有彈力即可。
* 麵糰放在已塗油之深盆中，以濕毛巾蓋着，置溫暖地方發1½小時至雙倍大。
* 將發起麵糰倒在已洒粉之桌上搓2分鐘，盡量將氣壓出。以手搓成圓條分為20等份，每份約重1安（28克）。將每份麵糰搓成圓形再按成

8吋（20公分）長條，頭尾兩端略粗。
* 將每條麵條絪成小結（參看圖片）放在已塗油之焗盤中置一旁再發約1小時。
* 焗爐預熱至350度（煤氣4度）。
* 每個包塗上蛋液放入焗爐中格焗約15分鐘，取出掃上糖膠即成。

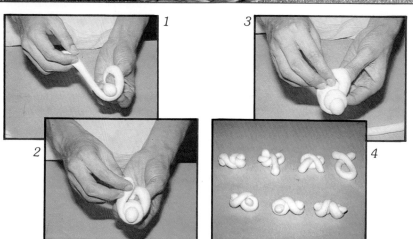

1

3

2

4

餐　　包　　仔
Fancy Buns

Ingredients:

Yeast Paste-
1/2 tsp sugar
1/2 cup warm water
1 1/4 tsp dry yeast
4 oz (112 g) high protein flour

Bread Dough-
1 lb (1/2 kg) high protein flour
1 egg
3 1/2 oz (98 g) sugar
2 1/2 tbsp milk
1/2 cup warm water
2 1/2 tbsp melted lard

To Finish-
1 beaten egg
1/4 cup light syrup
  for glazing

Method:

Yeast Paste-
* *Dissolve the sugar in the warm water. Sprinkle the dry yeast on top and leave in a warm place for 10 minutes until frothy.*
* *Sift in the high protein flour to stir into a paste. Leave until the mixture froths up.*

Bread Dough-
* *Sift the flour on to a table and make a well in the centre. Put the egg, sugar and yeast paste into the well to mix until the sugar dissolves. Gradually draw in the flour then add the milk and water to knead into a soft dough.*

Lastly knead in the lard. Stretch and pound against the table to ensure an even texture.
* *Put the dough in a greased mixing bowl and cover with a damp towel. Leave to rise in a warm place for about 1 1/2 hours until double in bulk.*
* *Turn the risen dough out of the bowl on to a floured board and knead lightly for 2 minutes to avoid a porey texture. Divide into 20 equal portions weighing 1 oz (28 g) each. Knead each into a smooth ball then roll into a round strip of 8" (20 cm) long with 2 ends thicker than the middle.*
* *Tie each strip into a knot (Refer to photographs) and return to a warm place to prove for 1 hour on a greased baking tray.*
* *Preheat the oven to 350°F (Gas Mark 4).*
* *Brush each bun with the beaten egg and bake for 15 to 20 minutes in the middle shelf of the oven. Remove the buns from the oven then glaze with the light syrup.*

橙 嗜 喱 圈
Orange Jelly Chiffon Ring

Ingredients:

Sponge ring-
3 eggs
1½ oz (42 g) sugar
2 drops vanilla essence
1 tbsp evaporated milk
2 oz (56 g) plain flour
1½ tbsp melted butter

Jelly-
1 packet orange flavoured jelly
1 cup boiling water
4 slices orange

Filling-
½ cup water
½ packet of orange jelly powder
1½ oz (42 g) sugar
½ oz (14 g) gelatine
3 oz (84 g) fresh cream
6 oz (168 g) mashed orange

Decoration-
1 cup fresh cream
a few slices orange
a few cherries

Method:

Sponge ring-
* Set oven at 350°F (Gas Mark 4).
* Beat the eggs with the sugar until fluffy. Drop in the vanilla essence and milk to mix well. Fold in the sieved flour then blend in the melted butter. Pour into a greased Paris ring mould and bake in the preheated oven for 20 minutes.

* Invert the cake and leave to cool on a cake rack. Remove and slice into 3 pieces. Clean and dry the cake mould for later use.

Jelly-
* Dissolve the jelly powder in the boiling water then leave to cool.
* Line the orange slices inside the cleaned Paris ring mould. Pour in the cold jelly and leave to set in the refrigerator.

Filling-
* Slowly bring the water to boil in a saucepan.
* Mix the orange jelly powder, sugar and gelatine together then pour into the boiling water to stir until dissolved. Sit the saucepan in a basin of crushed ice and leave to cool. Blend in the fresh cream and the mashed orange to whisk till half set.

To complete-
* Pour ⅓ of the filling on top of the orange jelly then top with a layer of the sponge ring. Repeat twice. Put in the refrigerator and leave to set. Invert on a platter to remove the cake mould. Decorate both sides of the ring by piping on the fresh cream with a rose nozzle, then arrange the orange slices and cherries on top of the jelly.

橙 啫 喱 圈
Orange Jelly Chiffon Ring

材料：

蛋糕—鷄蛋 3 隻
　　　糖 1½ 安（42克）
　　　香油 2 滴
　　　花奶 1 湯匙
　　　麵粉 2 安（56克）
　　　溶牛油 1½ 湯匙

啫喱—橙啫喱粉 1 包
　　　沸水 1 杯
　　　橙數片

夾心—水 ½ 杯
　　　橙啫喱粉 ½ 包
　　　糖 1½ 安（42克）
　　　魚膠粉 ½ 安（14克）
　　　鮮忌廉 3 安（84克）
　　　橙茸 6 安（168克）

裝飾—忌廉 1 杯唧花
　　　橙數片
　　　櫻桃數粒

製法：

蛋糕—
* 鷄蛋與糖同放蛋桶中打起，滴入香油及花奶打至輕軟。將已篩妥之麵粉倒在蛋液中拌勻，最後加入牛油和勻。傾入塗油圓環餅模內，置已預熱350度（煤氣4度）之焗爐中焗約18分鐘。
* 反轉在蛋糕架上攤凍，取出片成 3 件。

啫喱—
* 將啫喱粉溶於沸水中攤凍。
* 橙數片平均放在圓環糕盤內，傾入已攤凍之啫喱，置雪柜內雪實。

餡料—
* 水放鍋中慢慢煮沸。
* 橙啫喱粉，糖及魚膠粉撈勻，搞入沸水中，慢火煮片刻至各物溶化。坐在碎冰上至開始凝結時，將鮮忌廉及橙茸加入拌勻至半凝結。

完成—
* 將餡料三份之一倒在啫喱上，舖上一層蛋糕，重覆二次。放雪柜中雪凍，取出倒轉在碟上唧上鮮忌廉以橙片及櫻桃裝飾。

杏仁豆腐
Cold Almond Bean Curd

材料：

大菜½安（14克）
水8杯
糖1杯
花奶1杯
杏仁油1茶匙
什菓1大罐

製法：

* 大菜洗淨用清水浸片刻。
* 鍋中放水8杯，加入揸乾水份之大菜及糖一同煮溶。
* 離火加入花奶及杏仁油調勻。
* 用篩隔着將混合物傾在玻璃盆中，攤凍後放雪櫃內雪至凝結，取出切成四方粒。
* 將四方粒倒在玻璃兜內，加什菓拌勻，如不夠甜可加糖水半杯和勻。

Ingredients:

1/2 oz (14 g) agar agar
8 cups water
1 cup sugar
1 cup fresh milk
1 tsp almond essence
1 tin fruit cocktail

Method:

* *Wash, soak and drain the agar agar.*
* *Clean a 4-quart saucepan and pour in the water. Add the sugar and agar agar then bring to the boil. Simmer over low heat until both the ingredients are dissolved.*
* *Remove the saucepan from the stove then stir in the milk and almond essence.*
* *Filter the liquid through a sieve then leave to set. Cut into diamond shapes after it has solidfied. Place in a big bowl and pour the fruit cocktail on top.*
* *Mix evenly and serve in small bowls.*

上 湯 製 法
Chicken Stock

材料：

金華腿1磅（½公斤）
瘦肉1磅（½公斤）
豬骨1磅（½公斤）
老鷄1隻
水30杯

製法：

* 金華腿用沸水洗擦乾淨，與瘦肉，豬骨同放一鍋沸水中焓十分鐘，取出置水喉下冲洗。
* 老鷄用鹽擦淨，亦放沸水鍋中焓五分鐘，取出過凍水漂去脂肪。
* 預備深鍋一個，放入水30杯，將火腿、瘦肉、豬骨、老鷄全部放入，猛火煮沸後轉用文火續煮四小時，至餘下上湯8杯左右即可。
* 將上湯盛起，餘下肉渣可再放水4杯煮半小時作二湯用。

Ingredients:

1 lb (¹/₂ kg) Virginia ham
1 lb (¹/₂ kg) lean pork
1 lb (¹/₂ kg) bones
¹/₂ wok boiling water
1 old chicken
30 cups water

Method:

* *Scrub and clean the ham. Wash the pork and bones. Put the three ingredients into the boiling water to simmer for 10 minutes. Remove and rinse thoroughly. Keep the boiling water for later use.*
* *Remove and discard the chicken skin. Blanch the chicken in the boiling water for 5 minutes. Remove the excess oil from the chicken by rinsing it under a running tap.*
* *Pour the water into a deep saucepan. Put in the ham, pork, bones and chicken to bring to boil over high heat. Reduce to very low heat to simmer for about 4 hours until a quarter of the stock is left.*
* *Remove and filter the stock and leave aside for later use. Add another 4 cups of water to the sediments and simmer for a further 30 minutes. This can also be used as stock.*

酸甜醋製法
Sweet and Sour Sauce

材料：

米醋2杯
片糖或黃沙糖1杯
茄汁½杯
喼汁⅕杯
雞粉½茶匙
鹽⅕茶匙
花紅粉⅛茶匙

製法：

* 將米醋、片糖同置鍋內煮沸。
* 茄汁、喼汁及其他調味料加入續煮片刻。
* 將煮妥之混合物用茶隔隔去雜物後，放置瓶中攤凍。蓋上瓶蓋放雪櫃內可以久藏不壞。
* 用前搖勻，將所需份量用杯量妥放入鍋內煮沸，加豆粉水搞勻至自己要求之濃度。

Ingredients:

2 cups rice vinegar
1 cup brown sugar (packed)
1/2 cup tomato ketchup
1/5 cup Worchestershire sauce
1/2 tsp chicken powder
1/5 tsp salt
1/8 tsp red food colouring

Method:

* *Place the vinegar and the sugar into a saucepan and bring to the boil over low heat.*
* *Add the tomato ketchup and Worchestershire sauce with other ingredients to simmer for a while. Turn off the heat and leave to cool.*

* *Filter the solution before pouring into a jar. Keep for future use.*
* *Shake the jar before use. Pour the quantity needed into a saucepan and bring it to boil. Gradually stir in the cornflour mix to blend until smooth and thick.*

Chinese Cookery Terms

1. **To BAKE** is to cook with dry heat, or to dry food with heat.
2. **To BARBEQUE** is to cook meat over a charcoal or wood fire.
3. **To BIND** is to add egg, liquid or melted fat to a mixture in order to hold it together.
4. **To BLANCH** is to immerse the food in boiling water for a short time (from 10 seconds to 5 minutes) in order to tighten the texture, set the colour, or get rid of any unpleasant smell of the food.
5. **To BOIL** is to cook the food in hot bubbling liquid.
6. **To BRAISE** is to finish cooking in a tightly covered wok or saucepan.
7. **To CRIMP** is to slash the surface of a fish at intervals.
8. **To DEEP FRY** is to cook food in a large amount of hot boiling oil in order to make it crispy.
9. **To DOUBLE-BOIL** is to cook in a covered container, which is placed in a covered wok half-filled with boiling water.
10. **To DRAIN** is to remove excess liquid from the ingredients through a strainer or colander.
11. **To DREDGE** is to sprinkle the ingredient with flour or sugar, etc.
12. **To FRY** is to cook with a little hot oil.
13. **To GUT** is to remove the intestine and clean the inside of a fish.
14. **To PARBOIL** is to leave the food in warm oil until half-cooked.
15. **To PARCH** is to brown food in a dry hot wok or frying pan.
16. **To POACH** is to simmer food gently in a liquid which is kept just below boiling point.
17. **To REFRESH** is to rinse the ingredient with cold water after it is blanched. The ingredient is then reheated before serving.
18. **To ROAST** is to prepare the food by using high heat, with flame or over the charcoal.
19. **To SAUTÉ is to stir the ingredients quickly in a wok or pan with a little hot oil, over high heat.**
20. **To SCALD** is to plunge the ingredient into boiling water quickly to make peeling easier or to clean or loosen the hair on the ingredient.
21. **To SHALLOW FRY** is to cook the food in a little oil until both sides are brown.
22. **To SIMMER** is to cook the food or liquid slowly over low heat.
23. **To SMOKE** is to place the food on a rack in a wok or oven filled with smoke.
24. **To STEAM** is to cook the food by putting it into a steamer placed in a wok half-filled with boiling water. Timing begins when the water boils. High heat should be used so that there is enough steam to cook the food quickly.
25. **To STEW** is to cook the food with a little liquid over low heat.
26. **To STIR FRY** is to cook the food quickly in a little oil over medium heat.
27. **To TOSS** is to mix the ingredients evenly by throwing them in a wok and jerking the wok up and down.

The cooking oil used in this book can either be corn oil, vegetable oil, peanut oil or sunflower oil, unless otherwise stated.

烹飪常用術語

焗　—將食物放鑊中蓋密，以文火焗熟。或將拌妥粉料放焗爐中以慢火焗至鬆發。

炭燒　—將食物以叉叉着或放在炭上之鐵網直接以明火燒熟。

搞　—加水或蛋或牛奶在乾材料中和成一糰。

飛水　—將食物放入沸水內稍拖一下，取出洗淨續煮。

焓　—將食物放入沸水中，藉沸水熱力使食物煮熟。與灼及煮略同。灼要手快。

紅燒　—用豉油及水將食物煮熟。與煮及炆略同，有時則與烤之意義相近如燒烤。

炸　—將大量油煮沸，放入食物浸過面，以沸油之熱度使食物炸至酥脆。油炸食品多需上乾粉或濕粉，並要猛油落鑊。

燉　—將食物加配料及水放在燉盅內，再轉放深鍋中加水慢火燉至食品酥爛。食前加調味。此法可保原味，多與補品同燉。

上粉　—將食物以麵粉或糖洒勻在週圍而後按實。

炒　—將鑊燒紅，加少量油煮沸，放入材料迅速兜勻。

泡油　—將食物醃好後，放入猛鑊陰油中泡至油將沸時撈起，隔去油候用。

烙　—以燒熱乾鑊將已洗淨材料文火煮乾後續烙至淺黃色。

浸　—用湯或油煮沸後將火降至將沸未沸之溫度，把食物如鷄或魚等放入，以一定之溫度浸至熟，切不可用猛火。

過冷河　—將食物先用沸水煮過，取出再放冷水中冲凍使其爽脆，麵食多須過冷河。

烤　—以明火將食物炙熟使香氣四溢，用中式烤爐與西式焗爐皆可。

爆　—迅速用猛火將食物以油或醬料加料頭用火逼熟。

灼或燙　—將食物迅速放入沸水中浸片刻然後去皮或拔毛。

煎　—燒紅鑊放少量油將食物僅浸到少許，慢火煎至兩面金黃香脆。

燴　—燒熱油鑊，瓚酒加上湯，再加已泡油或煮熟之食物及配料煮沸，以粟粉開水少許打饙。

烟或燻　—食物先用調味品醃過，排在已放燻料（糖、蔗片、茶葉等）之鑊中的鐵絲網上。蓋上鑊蓋，藉燻料冒出之烟使食物燻至微黃而有烟味。

蒸　—將食物以碟盛起放蒸籠內蓋密，轉置沸水鑊中以蒸氣使食物致熟。

炆　—先將食物放配料爆炒過，轉放另一密蓋鑊內加水少許，改用文火經長時間炆至食物酥爛汁濃爲止。紅炆者熟後加老抽。

拌炒　—此爲中國烹飪中最常用之方法，將食物先泡嫩油至七分熟，然後再燒紅鑊加配料放食物瓚酒，迅速兜勻上碟。

拋　—將鑊中食物迅速在大火上拋動，使火力平均。

煮　—將食物放入水中煮，藉沸水之熱力將食品煮至酥爛，然後加調味料。

煲　—將食物放入水中煮滾，改用文火繼續保至夠火及出味爲止。此法通常需時較長。

滷　—用水加滷水料、生抽、紹酒、冰糖等煮至出味。然後把食物飛水後浸在鹵水中。浸至入味。滷水盆如處理得宜可長期不變壞。

煨　—將食物放入上湯內慢火煮之，使其吸收上湯味道，或放羗葱水內煨之，以除腥味。

撈拌　—把已煮熟之食物切絲與其他配料放在一起和勻謂之撈。多用於冷盆。

扒　—手法與燴略同，唯汁水較少及較濃。

註：本書食譜內所用之油通常爲粟米油，亦可用菜油或花生油。

MEAT MARINADE

Seasoning used / 1 lb (½ kg) of meat	Sugar	Light Soy	Soda Bi-carbonate	Egg White	Cornflour	Wine
🐷	1 tbsp	2 tbsp			1 tbsp	1 tbsp
🐄	1 tbsp	2 tbsp	1½ tsp		1 tbsp	1 tbsp
🐐	1 tbsp	2 tbsp	1 tsp		1 tbsp	1 tbsp
🐔	1 tbsp	1 tbsp		1	1 tbsp	2 tbsp
🪿	1 tbsp	2 tbsp	1 tsp	1	1 tbsp	2 tbsp
🦆	1 tbsp	2 tbsp	2 tsp		1 tbsp	2 tbsp
🕊️	1 tsp	1 tbsp		1	1 tbsp	1 tbsp
🐟	1 tbsp	2 tbsp		1	1 tbsp	
🦐				1	2 tbsp	

Ginger Juice	Pepper	Water	Method	Oil	Total Marinate Time
	⅛ tsp	⅓ cup	Mix and leave for 30 minutes	¼ cup	1 hour
	¼ tsp	1 cup	Mix and leave for 1 hour	⅓ cup	2 hours
1 tbsp	¼ tsp	½ cup	Mix and leave for 1 hour	¼ cup	2 hours
2 tbsp	⅛ tsp	⅓ cup	Mix and leave for 10 minutes	⅓ cup	½ hour
2 tbsp	¼ tsp	½ cup	Mix and leave for 1 hour	⅓ cup	2 hours
2 tbsp	¼ tsp	½ cup	Mix and leave for 1 hour	½ cup	2 hours
1 tbsp	⅛ tsp	⅓ cup	Mix and leave for 10 minutes	¼ cup	½ hour
1 tbsp	¼ tsp		Mix		½ hour
	⅛ tsp		Mix		10 minutes

各種肉類醃料份量及時間

調味 1磅 ($\frac{1}{2}$公斤) 肉類	糖	生抽	鬆肉粉	蛋白	生粉	酒
🐷	1湯匙	2湯匙			1湯匙	1湯匙
🐮	1湯匙	2湯匙	1$\frac{1}{2}$茶匙		1湯匙	1湯匙
🐐	1湯匙	2湯匙	1茶匙		1湯匙	1湯匙
🐔	1湯匙	1湯匙		1	1湯匙	2湯匙
🐤	1湯匙	2湯匙	1茶匙	1	1湯匙	2湯匙
🦆	1湯匙	2湯匙	2茶匙		1湯匙	2湯匙
🕊	1茶匙	1湯匙		1	1湯匙	1湯匙
🐟	1湯匙	2湯匙		1	1湯匙	
🦐				1	2湯匙	

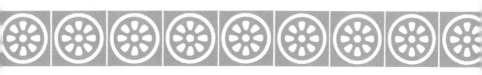

羌汁	胡椒粉	水	方法	油	時間
	$\frac{1}{8}$茶匙	$\frac{1}{3}$杯	拌勻, 置一旁醃30分鐘	$\frac{1}{4}$杯	1 小時
	$\frac{1}{4}$茶匙	1 杯	拌勻, 置一旁醃1 小時	$\frac{1}{3}$杯	2 小時
1 湯匙	$\frac{1}{4}$茶匙	$\frac{1}{2}$杯	拌勻, 置一旁醃1 小時	$\frac{1}{4}$杯	2 小時
2 湯匙	$\frac{1}{8}$茶匙	$\frac{1}{3}$杯	拌勻, 置一旁醃10分鐘	$\frac{1}{3}$杯	$\frac{1}{2}$小時
2 湯匙	$\frac{1}{4}$茶匙	$\frac{1}{2}$杯	拌勻, 置一旁醃1 小時	$\frac{1}{3}$杯	2 小時
2 湯匙	$\frac{1}{4}$茶匙	$\frac{1}{2}$杯	拌勻, 置一旁醃1 小時	$\frac{1}{2}$杯	2 小時
1 湯匙	$\frac{1}{8}$茶匙	$\frac{1}{3}$杯	拌勻, 置一旁醃10分鐘	$\frac{1}{4}$杯	$\frac{1}{2}$小時
1 湯匙	$\frac{1}{4}$茶匙		拌勻		$\frac{1}{2}$小時
	$\frac{1}{8}$茶匙		拌勻		10分鐘

Our Cooking Centre

Chinese Cookery Courses

Chinese Dishes Course
Chinese Roasts Course
Dim Sum Course
Cakes & Pastries Course
Professional Bread-making Course
Bean Curd Course
Moon Cake Course
Piping Course
Wedding Cake Course
Ingredients Course
Banquet Dishes Course
Vegetable Carving Course
Deep Fried Pastry Course

* * * * * * *

½-3 days Tourist Group Course
1 day Selected Course
1-week Tourist Course
4-week Intensive Course
8-week Intensive Course
13-week Professional Course
17-week Teacher Training Course

Length of course:–
　　　2 hours to 17 weeks

Our Hostel

* Air-conditioning
* Colour T.V.
* Private bath
* Private telephone
* Reasonable rent

3-DAY TOURIST GROUP COURSE

US$300.00 per head for a group of 10 to 15 persons
Schedule as follows–

Time	Day 1	Day 2	Day 3
10 am	2 Chinese dishes	2 Chinese dishes	Market Visit
12 noon	A taste of Chinese dishes	A taste of dim sum	2 dish sum
2 pm	2 dim sum	2 Chinese dishes	2 dim sum
4 pm	Chinese dish practice	Chinese dish practice	Chinese dish practice

嘉饌家政中心暫時尚未在任何國家開設分校。

各式烹飪班

各省中菜班
初高燒烤班
初高點心班
高級西餅班
職業麵包班
馳名豆腐班
速成月餅班
速成啷花班
結婚禮餅班
各式原料班
筵席大菜班
蔬菓雕花班
各式油器班
1/2—3天集體遊客班
1天各科精選班
1週遊客班
4週速成班
8週速成班
13週職業班
17週教師訓練班

專業烹飪導師培訓班
學制分1年，2年及3年
基本移民班
高級移民班

宿舍設備

＊空氣調節
＊彩色電視
＊私家浴室
＊私人電話
＊合理價錢

"CHOPSTICKS RECIPES"

is a symbol of   CONFIDENCE

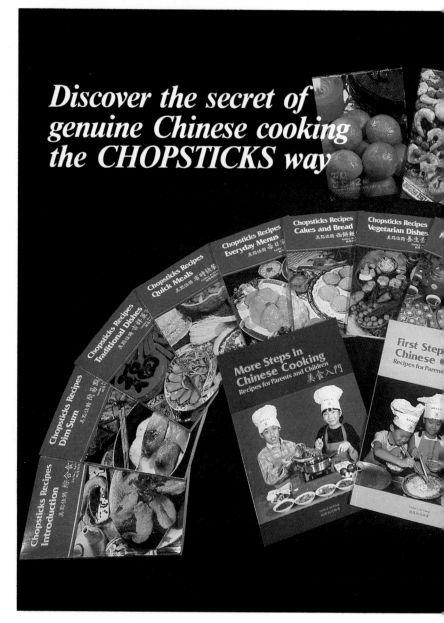

Discover the secret of genuine Chinese cooking the CHOPSTICKS way

CHOPSTICKS PUBLICATIONS
a symbol of confidence

The **Chopsticks Recipes** series English-Chinese bilingual edition (128 pp 105 gsm matt art paper) is an encyclopedia to Chinese cuisine, written for people who enjoy trying different kinds of Chinese food in their daily life. Book 1 is an introduction to a variety of cooking while each of the other 11 books contain one specific subject.

Book 1 — introduction
Book 2 — Dim Sum
Book 3 — Traditional Dishes
Book 4 — Quick Meals
Book 5 — Everyday Menus
Book 6 — Cakes and Bread
Book 7 — Vegetarian Dishes
Book 8 — More Dim Sum
Book 9 — Budget Meals
Book 10 — Chinese Casseroles
Book 11 — Healthy Bean Dishes
Book 12 — Vegetable Carvings

First Steps in Chinese Cooking and **More Steps in Chinese Cooking** English-Chinese bilingual edition (96 pp 115 gsm matt art paper) each contains 42 specially written recipes which have been tested by children from the ages of 8 to 14 years. These book are designed for parents and children to learn Chinese cooking together.

Other Chopsticks publications include
Chopsticks Cookery Cards Grades 1 and 2 English-Chinese bilingual edition (260 gsm B/S coated art board with pp lamination)

Chopsticks Recipes revised English Edition (128 pp 128 gsm matt art paper)

Chopsticks Wok Miracles English-Chinese bilingual edition (128 pp 128 gsm matt art paper)

海外訂書價目表
OVERSEAS MAIL ORDER FORM

Cookery Books

Revised Chopsticks Recipes (Bilingual edition)

_____ copies Book 1 - Introduction 綜合食譜 @ US$7.95 =US$ _____
_____ copies Book 2 - Dim Sum 簡易點心 @ US$7.95 =US$ _____
_____ copies Book 3 - Traditional Dishes 吉祥菜譜 @ US$7.95 =US$ _____
_____ copies Book 4 - Quick Meals 省時快餐 @ US$7.95 =US$ _____
_____ copies Book 5 - Everyday Menus 每日菜譜 @ US$7.95 =US$ _____
_____ copies Book 6 - Cakes and Bread 西餅麵包 @ US$7.95 =US$ _____
_____ copies Book 7 - Vegetarian Dishes 養生素食 @ US$7.95 =US$ _____
_____ copies Book 8 - More Dim Sum 南北點心 @ US$7.95 =US$ _____
_____ copies Book 9 - Budget Meals 經濟小菜 @ US$7.95 =US$ _____
_____ copies Book 10 - Chinese Casseroles 瓦鍋食譜 @ US$7.95 =US$ _____
_____ copies Book 11 - Healthy Bean Dishes 豆類食譜 @ US$7.95 =US$ _____
_____ copies Book 12 - Vegetable Carvings 蔬果雕花 @ US$9.95 =US$ _____

Chopsticks Recipes (English Edition)

_____ copies Revised Book 1 - Introduction @ US$7.95 =US$ _____

Chopsticks Cookery Cards for Beginners (Bilingual Edition)

_____ sets Cookery Cards - Grade 1 美食初階(1) @ US$4.00 =US$ _____
_____ sets Cookery Cards - Grade 2 美食初階(2) @ US$4.00 =US$ _____

Chopsticks Wok Miracles (Bilingual Edition)

_____ copies Book 1 美鑊飄香(1) @ US$7.95 =US$ _____

Children Cookery Books (Bilingual Edition)

_____ copies First Steps in Chinese Cooking 美食入門(1) @ US$9.95 =US$ _____
_____ copies More Steps in Chinese Cooking 美食入門(2) @ US$9.95 =US$ _____

Art Books

_____ copies 'The World of Bu Di' art album 卜鏑畫册 @ US$40.00 =US$ _____
_____ sets Bu Di's Painting Cards 卜鏑畫卡每套8張 @ US$3.00 =US$ _____
Registered Postage & Packing for_____ copies/sets =US$ _____
TOTAL =US$ _____

I enclosed a bankdraft of US$_____ , crossed and made payable to
CHOPSTICKS PUBLICATIONS LTD. 支票抬頭請寫

Name : _____
Address: _____
Please return to : Chopsticks Publications Ltd.
Kowloon Central P.O. Box 73515
Kowloon, HONG KONG

Registered Surface Postage and Packing for 掛號海郵(20本以上免郵費)

1 to 3 items............US$6.00   4 to 6 items...................US$9.00
7 to 19 items.........US$16.00   20 items plus...........postage free
Extra postage for the World of Bu Di...US$4.00